THE DREADFUL CONSEQUENCES
OF THINKING LIKE A
THEIST!

Elliot George dissects Dr Andy Bannister's book
THE ATHEIST WHO DIDN'T EXIST
(or The Dreadful Consequences of Bad Arguments)

Illustrations by Sebastian

When I was an Afairyist,
I went out with an Agoblinist girl.
It didn't work out...
We had no disbeliefs in common !

ACKNOWLEDGEMENTS

I am deeply indebted to Dr Andy Bannister for inspiring me to write this book. He has spurred me into getting my thoughts in order for addressing the many erroneous ways of thinking that enable theists to think they have justification for believing in a 'god'. I am also preparing a forty-minute presentation to cover this subject. Interested? Contact: elliotgeorge666@gmail.com

I am seriously grateful to Sebastian for his wonderful illustrations that really lift our work above the ordinary text-only books into a realm of reader-friendly infotainment.

I owe immense gratitude to:
Paul Brocklehurst for his early encouragement and suggestions.
Brian Hallin, John Herrick, Diana Langley and Vivienne Rathband for proof reading.
A young man with a glittering career ahead of him, Alex J O'Connor (Cosmic Skeptic), for the well crafted Foreword.

FOREWORD

by Alex O'Connor (YouTube's 'Cosmic Skeptic')

The book you hold in your hands contains little justification for its criticisms of religion, and for good reason. I have never fully understood the hypocrisy exhibited in the ability of certain individuals to freely and unapologetically challenge anything they feel contradicts their *own* corrupt visions of science and society, and yet then expect some moral excuse when anybody attempts to disagree with them. 'Why should you want to take away something that brings hope to billions of people?' 'What gives you the right to insult my prophet?' 'Why do you hate religious people?' If you are beginning, as I am, to tire of the repetition apparent in the numerous works of prominent atheist writers and speakers, consider for a moment the fact that a repetition of arguments against a claim requires a repetition of arguments *in favor* of that claim. It has been said that no serious evidence has been proposed in favor of atheism in decades, perhaps even centuries, and every time this case is put to me, I can't help but cringe at the blood pouring from the accuser's foot, especially given that they are usually completely oblivious of having so embarrassingly shot it in the first place. This is a simple issue of burden of proof. Neatly covered in the following first chapter is the fact that atheists, on the whole, have nothing to prove. Of course, atheists who make active claims such as 'there are no gods' and 'science can explain everything' do exist and those claims do require some proof. However, whilst both of these statements certainly require the person from whom they originate to be an atheist, *atheism does not require the acceptance of these statements.* The word atheism comes from a coalescence of the Greek 'a-' meaning without, and 'theos' meaning god. You need not actively disbelieve in the existence of gods to be an atheist: *it is enough to simply be skeptical of the opposite belief and to live without the influence of any deity.* That is to say, people who set out to challenge religion are almost always doing exactly that - challenging a set of beliefs, not presenting their own set of beliefs that needs its own complimentary set of defenses.

In recognizing this, the irony of the claim that no decent argument has been recently presented in favor of atheism becomes piercingly apparent. If the goal of an advocate for atheism is to rebut the assertions of religious claims, then his points will consist of responses to those put forward by religious apologists. Therefore, if there have been no new arguments against the existence of gods in any number of years, that is because there have been no new arguments *in favor* of the existence of gods in the same time. This isn't to say that there haven't been attempts made in the modern era; one example of such is the 'fine tuning' argument (I have added the quotation marks because the universe is in no way finely tuned for the existence of Homo sapiens). Inevitably,

4

such attempts always crumble under the most rudimentary scrutiny, and the theist is once again forced to resort to the traditional moral objections that pervade this particular branch of philosophical debate and have done for at least the past few centuries. Among these fatuous objections are the quoted examples given above, which all share a depressing essence of despondence, in that they suggest that religion is all that some people have. If you are somebody who would lose all hope, meaning and enthusiasm for life if your god did not exist, then you are missing out on the many and often superior alternative sources for these comforts that are at your disposal, and I would suggest that you promptly begin to explore them, as truth has a tendency to become progressively more apparent and convincing, even if you'd prefer that it didn't.

Whilst I am certainly not unsympathetic (and am in fact empathetic) towards the kind of people who feel deeply troubled by the possibility that they have wasted a significant portion of their lives praying to and worshipping a non-existent entity, I maintain that, ultimately, a worldview based on science and reason is endlessly more fulfilling than one based on any theology. Furthermore, though it may outrage you to have your religious views questioned and criticized, this is not a sufficient reason for anybody to cease their investigations of reality. Attempts made to evaluate supernatural claims need no more of a warrant than the innate desire that exists within all rational creatures to pursue truth wherever it leads. They need no more of a warrant than do attempts to evaluate political ideologies, or does the criticism of film, music, art or poetry. This book is the product of no ulterior motives, no suspicious intentions, and exploitative goals, but rather an innocent and admirable desire to understand the world in which we have all been generously granted our limited time.

I say generously not to imply some generous creator, but instead to stress just how lucky you and I are to be here, on this imperfect planet of ours. To a believer in the afterlife, our worldly existence is but a preliminary phase, and the lives we lead here will eventually be lost and forgotten to the boundless eternity that awaits us, making them almost not worth living. To the rest of us, however, this life is all that we have, and whilst we may also believe that it will ultimately be forgotten to time, this only makes it all the more enjoyable, and worth living without the superfluous interference of any false hopes. If, then, you find yourself unnerved by the contents of the following pages, consider it not as the beginning of a purposeless life, but rather as a step towards the philosophically autonomous existence that you deserve.

October 2017 Oxford

PREFACE

Don't get me wrong.

This book is not intended to be an attack on Dr Andy Bannister. On the contrary, I admire and like him. I particularly like the way he *doesn't* keep quoting the Bible! Andy's writing is easily readable. He's a great creative author. He might make a good novelist. As for me, I try to write in an accessible style, as befits a retired science teacher[1].

Andy and I are kindred spirits in many ways. We are both Englishmen. We both have young families. We both write books. We have both appeared on the same Christian radio station, we both contribute to internet forums and speak in live debates. In my online exchanges with Andy, he has come across as a very well read person whose intention is to interact in a gentlemanly way. We may appear together touring a live gladiatorial dialogue event. Would you like to see that? If so please contact elliotgeorge666@gmail.com

So, going by the Skeptics in the Pub[2] motto of 'Respect People: Challenge Ideas', what I *am* doing is questioning the 'conclusions'[3] that Andy and others have come to in their deliberations about their Christian faith. To be more specific, I do not consider them to *be* conclusions; they are just wishful hypotheses[4]. Please read on to find out more...

"What the world needs more than ever is a reasonable dialogue between those who believe in God and those who have questions or doubts (however deeply held), not a clash of fundamentalisms"
Dr Andy BANNISTER

~~~

"Andy, how can anyone be a DOUBTFUL fundamentalist?
Isn't fundamentalism all about utter conviction?
And isn't 'the clash' between DIFFERENT FAITHS?
Hasn't it always been?
Look at history.
Watch The News."

CONTENTS

PART ONE:
THE DEMOLITION OF BELIEF SYSTEMS
(Christianity in particular)

1. INTRODUCTION

Firstly, I'm not an 'atheist'.

That's a theists' word for those who *don't* belong – a spurious category if ever there was one! It's like saying, "All creatures *without feathers*, from snails to giraffes should be *grouped together into one class and called the 'Abirds'!*"

THE ABIRDS

So, the *very title* of The Atheist Who Didn't Exist is the first of many fallacies in Andy's book (it's a False Assumption). However, it would be foolish to deny the existence of the word 'atheist' so I shall employ it, but always in quotation marks, to indicate its uselessness.

It is currently not possible to be absolutely sure that there are no 'gods' (let's take 'god' to mean 'creator deity') because the universe is too big to search and, therefore, there can be no 100% *certain* 'atheists'. Quixotically[5], Andy is tilting at windmills if he imagines that there are lots of 'atheists', one of whom doesn't exist! Of course, that is not what he wishes to say: he is *trying to be clever* and imply that 'atheism' is not a valid worldview. He's almost right – it's not *even* a worldview.

So what *am* I? I'm a non-believer in 'gods'. Think of it like this: if you don't have a dollar, you just lack cash and that's that.

SORRY! I'M CLEAN OUT OF GODS RIGHT NOW...

Sebastian

Theists often change the meanings of words and for them 'atheist' is a useful insult to hurl at the motley collection of the non-religious. It's a denigrating label for castigating those who don't *belong*. It's for promoting **atheistophobia**[6]. Historically, 'heathen', 'gentile' and 'infidel' have been used for the same disrespectful purpose. Personally, I wouldn't describe myself as an 'atheist' – that's just playing into the theists' hands.

Early in his book, Andy says,

"What the world needs more than ever is a reasonable dialogue between those who believe in God and those who have questions or doubts (however deeply held), not a clash of fundamentalisms"

I agree with Andy that reasonable dialogue is preferable to a clash of fundamentalisms. Ask yourself, who *wouldn't* be in favor of civil discourse and rational discussion? However, I am puzzled by his implication that non-belief can *be* a fundamentalism. It's not even an '-ism': that's usually the suffix for an ideology or belief system.

13

All faiths are ideologies; they have values and principles that they compel us to adopt, *and* they have a mission to recruit more members. 'Atheism' has none of that, but it suits believers to construct an image of 'atheism' as a belief system and then to attack what they *imagine* is its ideology. Theists understand '-isms' because they are familiar with the doctrines of their personal theism *and* they are used to disagreeing with believers of *other* theisms. So calling non-belief an '-ism' gives them a target they are used to aiming at and keeps them in their comfort zone by imposing their style of worldview on to 'atheists' (it's the Mind Projection Fallacy[7]).

However, 'atheism' *isn't* an ideology. It has no doctrines. It's merely a negative stance on a single issue. It just inherited its '-ism' ending from the parent word: 'theism'. 'Atheists' lack belief in gods, period. Creating an ideology around 'atheism' is like trying to give a hairstyle to the naturally bald. The bald don't need combs, and 'atheists' don't need a system of religious taboos and tenets, they don't need to join a hierarchical organization just to say, *"I'm not sure that's true."*

AND HOW WOULD SIR LIKE IT TODAY?

14

There are lots of instances of *lack* like this. For example, you don't need a recipe to make no cake; at age nought we have zero education; innocence (guiltlessness) is presumed, it's guilt that has to be proven, and so on. It would be ridiculous to assume that vegetarians or teetotalers have scriptures and doctrines, wouldn't it? According to theists' bizarre way of thinking, my habit of deliberately *never* gambling would make me into a fundamental *Agamblerist!*

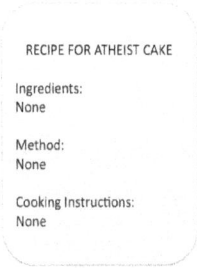

RECIPE FOR ATHEIST CAKE

Ingredients:
None

Method:
None

Cooking Instructions:
None

ET VOILÀ!

Absences do not spawn ideologies, nor do you need a counter ideology to reject a belief. All you need is skepticism: a standard for being convinced that requires positive evidence for a proposition. So, 'atheism' is really just a bad name for not believing in a god. Maybe Andy's title, 'The Atheist Who Didn't Exist', might best be taken as ironic because very few *real* 'atheists', in the sense of active disbelievers, actually do exist; people who describe themselves as 'atheists' are asserting their position with an unjustifiable level of certainty.

We can't be sure that the statement *"There is a god"* is false, so a better name for 'god' deniers would be 'anti-theists'.

Most non-believers are simply not persuaded by theists' claims, but that wouldn't suit Andy's purpose. You can't go up against something unless you have first polarized the playing field to identify your opponents. White plays black not grey! In Andy's eyes, 'fence-sitting non-believers' must be properly blackened! He wants to attack people who rashly claim they are *certain* there is no god - *'fundamental doubters'!*

Etymologically, 'atheist' translates as 'without god'[8], which is the state we are *all* in, until 'god' has become an evidential reality. Yes, theists, *you* lack 'god' also. You are 'atheists' in that you are unavoidably 'without god' too, until you can produce evidence for your chosen 'god'.

Andy would probably agree that we are all without Zeus... Why would he do that? Would it be because of a lack of *evidence* for Zeus? Do Zeusians only have belief to go on? Is belief not evidence? We are not without *gravity*, but we *are* without evidential *'gods'*. If there are no gods, there can be no justifiable theists and the notion of 'atheist' becomes a nonsense. Since there's no evidence for the existence of a 'god' to deny, 'atheism' is a lack of belief in an absence! 'Atheism' is just a theist's Aunt Sally – a dummy target to throw wet sponges at.

So why do I only *'sort of'* agree with Andy's statement? In case you have forgotten, I mean this sentence:

"What the world needs more than ever is a reasonable dialogue between those who believe in God and those who have questions or doubts (however deeply held), not a clash of fundamentalisms"

I love the risible notion of *'those who have deeply held doubts'!* Members of 'IF' – the *Indecisive Fundamentalists!*

17

Or the *dogmatically dubious!*

Secondly, Andy's declaration contains a contentious presumption: that the world's population is divided into believers (specifically believers in the *Christian* god, the only *true* one as far as Andy is concerned) and *"those who have questions or doubts...however deeply held"*

Doubt doesn't inspire action let alone *tribal* behavior and so there are no doubters' organizations, least of all any radicalized fundamentalist doubters! Hands up all those who have had the Dubious  Jehovah Witnesses[9] calling at their door on a recruitment drive. Anyone? No? I thought not...

Andy is assuming that there is a polarity between *all* theists on the one hand and *all* non-believers on the other. Theists form communities but 'atheists' don't, so that's an example of the Fallacy of False Equivalence.[10] This way of thinking is encouraged by the very existence of the word 'atheist'. Labeling people as some sort of '-ists' makes it sound as though there really *is* an association that they belong to, with a constitution and a remit. Wouldn't we think that 'Smokerists' had a mission to make us smoke? I wonder where *members of other faiths* fit into Andy's polarized scenario? Does he group them with the 'atheists' or with the Christians?

The truth is that 'atheists' have no more in common than non-believers in Santa Claus or the Tooth Fairy do. 'We' don't share any doctrines to promote so 'we' are not really a 'we'. This is another example of the Mind Projection Fallacy. You don't see 'us' walking the streets wearing sandwich boards proclaiming 'Join Atheism' or seizing opportunities to pontificate at Speakers' Corner like Andy tells us he did. 'We' don't meet up every week to 're-affirm' our non-belief in the virgin birth! 'We' have no mission to convert the entire world round to believing in our (non-existent) ideology. What is there for 'atheists' to believe in? That's a preposterous notion because those are the activities of *believers*, people who are *driven* by a shared ideology, by shared values and principles. Ask yourself, who has ever been driven by doubt?

19

Doubt is the enemy of belief, the cause of *apathy not action*. Having *no shared cause* means 'atheists' do not congregate together and collect donations for communal projects like building halls for worship. Maybe 'we' *should* ask for 'offerings' and become rich but, if 'we' could, the funds would be taxable, unlike church funds! Perhaps the fledgling Sunday Assembly will develop a large following one-day...

The spread of science education and the reputation of science for answering questions are perceived as threats by some believers. An alternative source of explanations is competition for religions, especially when the rival answers have a track record for accuracy! So that is likely to be what has prompted Andy to bundle together all non-believers as the opponents. In reality, being 'The Excluded' rather than a coherent group means that 'atheists' are *not* organized and, therefore, cannot be accused of dividing humanity and causing conflict. Most non-believers are not scientists, nor are they interested in refuting the assorted faiths that the various theists believe in. Non-believers are not bent on imposing their, non-existent, 'ungodly principles' on the entire population. Instead, they tend to get on with their own business, humoring and tolerating everyone. When you *don't have a doctrine*, no-one can challenge it, so you have no disagreeable folk to hate. Ask yourself, isn't that obvious?

Many of us are familiar with other words prefixed by 'a'. Asexual means *without* sex, acellular means *without* cells, apolitical means *without* a political party affiliation, etc. The confusion about 'atheism' stems from the very word 'a-theism' itself. 'Atheism' is the antonym of 'theism'. Theism is an *ideology*, so it's an easy mistake to make to think of 'atheism' as an *opposite* ideology. Actually it just means *without* the ideology of *any* theism.

The reality is it's silly to categorize people on the basis of *a shared lack*. It's like herding together all innocent men and labeling them 'Aguilty'! Ask yourself, what would they have in common? Is this the reason why we don't have any 'A' prefixed ideologies: no 'Asocialism', 'Acommunism' or Aliberalism? We don't have them *because they don't make any sense!* Is Andy manufacturing a Straw Man because he wants to pick a fight with a particular type of adversary?

Dear reader, are you beginning to see the amount of work involved in addressing *just the title (The Atheist Who Didn't Exist) and one sentence* of Andy's book in an attempt to unravel it and make it match reality? Twelve pages! I'm exhausted already! *All of this because Andy wants to pick a fight with people whom he, rightfully, claims don't exist!*

My apologies in advance, but I won't be dealing with Andy's manuscript line by line; it's doubtful whether I would live long enough! The workings of the theistic mind are so completely at odds with a science teacher's thinking in such amazingly complex ways that it isn't possible to come up with simple concise responses. So, this book, while being *inspired* by The Atheist Who Didn't Exist, won't be merely a detailed critique of Andy's work. Rather, I shall use it as an opportunity to show readers how to think skeptically and critically. I hope you enjoy the journey from the demolition of Belief Systems to the construction of a Rational Worldview.

Jehovah's Witnesses don't celebrate Halloween
They don't appreciate random people coming up to their door.
Imtiaz MAHMOOD

Atheism is not a philosophy; it is not even a view of the world;
it is simply a refusal to deny the obvious.
Sam HARRIS

2. PROTECTING THEISM

Let's take a look at this famous quote by Stephen F. Roberts,

"I contend we are both atheists, I just believe in one less god than you do. When you understand why you dismiss all the other possible gods, you will understand why I dismiss yours."

Christian apologists protest that this reasoning doesn't apply to *their* 'god'. They claim it's a category error since their 'god' is a *justified true belief* (see later for what this is supposed to mean) while, they assert, all the other 'gods' are *obviously* false so *of course* it's right to disbelieve in them! They make their declaration of exclusive truth in the absence of any evidence. Meanwhile, believers of other faiths, also without evidence, are saying that the Christian's 'god' is the false one. They are making contradictory claims! What do you think?

The early Bible writers obviously perceived this problem of competition from the plethora of other 'gods' available at the time because they tried to combat it by issuing 'Commandments', with the first one being the assertion that:

I am the LORD thy God

and the next four being instructions that thou shalt:

Have no other gods but me
Have no graven images or likenesses
Not take the LORD's name in vain
Remember the Sabbath day

The Commandment authors obviously gave a higher priority to safeguarding their doctrine, *and therefore their income,* than to issuing advice on how to minimize disruptive behavior in society. Not until Commandment number six[11] (Honor thy mother and thy father) does anything appear that is remotely useful for fostering a well-ordered and peaceful community. Meanwhile murder is *relegated to number seven* (shouldn't it come first?) and there is no mention at all of malicious bodily harm or rape! Ask yourself, were the Commandments written by bullying, misogynistic men who didn't want anyone to wreck their control, ruin their income and spoil their fun? Well, were they?

We disbelieve the beliefs of others all the time, so why do we think our *own* beliefs are true? Don't we know that, to them, *we* are the others? Right there, is the problem with religions: they're *divisive.*[12] Division leads to disagreement, to demonization and, ultimately, to conflict. Couple this with the fact that there is no evidence for any 'god', *including yours,* plus they all have an mission to convert all of mankind to their *own* faith and you will see that, on balance, religions cause more harm than good. And they do that harm *needlessly,* because *all* 'gods' are just *hypothetical.*

The theist's backwards way of thinking about non-belief, which I call Contrary Cognition, leads to many problems especially when the incorrect assumption that "Atheism is an ideology" is coupled with the equally false claim that it takes a 'god' to bestow moral behavior (more about that in Chapter 7). The combination of those two erroneous concepts enables fundamental theists to demonize non-believers with accusations of immorality and the motivation to commit inhumane acts. It can be used as a 'justification' for the hating and victimizing of supposed 'heathens', 'gentiles' or 'infidels'. Non-belief, demonized by theists into 'Atheism', makes a useful weapon for protecting their non-evidential beliefs.

Worse still, this deadly duo of miss-beliefs enables theists to think they can point to genocidal dictators[13] like Stalin, Mao

Zhe Dong and Pol Pot and gloat, *"See, they were 'atheists',
look what they did!"* Well, they *were* megalomaniacs but their
motivation was the selfish acquisition of power, not 'atheism'.
Yet Andy says:

*When we look at Stalin's actions, his atheism seems quite
central.*

And he quotes Stalin saying this:

*"You know, they are fooling us, there is no god. All this talk
about god is sheer nonsense."*

OK, that may have been Stalin's *opinion* of faiths, but he does
not say that it was the *incentive for his actions*. Communism
was an anti-establishment movement that was against *all* the
previous power bases of the nobility *and the churches*
because the rebels wished to replace the old authorities with
submission to *the people's party and its leader*. Stalin was not
driven by 'atheism', but by *megalomania* like any demagogue.
It just happened to be convenient to make use of Russian
'atheists' as affiliates to his aspiration; the repression of
religion in China by Mao Tse Tung was also an attempt to
focus attention on the state national party.

Think about it, how can an *absence* be inspiring? Has any
motivational speaker ever offered *nothing* as the reward for

success in a sales drive or recruitment campaign? Ask yourself, are 'atheist' dictators supposed to be incentivized to please a deity who, they believe, *probably doesn't exist?*

Once you grasp that Andy is conflating 'atheism' with communism, you will see the folly of his position. And when you realize that non-believers are *not* a group and have no mission to recruit followers[14] in an attempt to take control of the entire world at the expense of all the major religions, you'll begin to see that Andy's book is addressing a foe of theists' own creation: the 'atheist', a Straw Man[15].

~~~

Anyone who has thrown off the vestments of their faith soon finds out that what they have joined is...................*nothing!*

So I contend that 'The Atheist Who Didn't Exist' consists largely of Straw Man arguments intended to confirm the presuppositions and biases of the author to himself. Andy is obviously thinking about his belief system and doubting it; he may be coming to realize that It needs some buttressing! I applaud such public self-examination and admire him for it.

~~~

Bertrand Russell once wrote,

"We cannot have reason to reject a belief except on the ground of some other belief."

Well, it may be bold of me, but I think Bertrand was wrong: *skepticism* should be enough reason to lack belief. Do we need to believe in goblins in order to reject fairies? But, if he is right, my 'other belief' is that beliefs are merely claims that should be confirmed by evidence before they become 'concrete facts'. At which point, ironically, they cease to need actively believing! This puts belief in its rightful place of *dubious claim*. Say after me, *"Oh, That's merely a belief is it?"*

Doesn't humanity need to escape from these ancient, divisive, groundless doctrines originating in a time of profound ignorance and vicious territorial conflict? If this is hurting your worldview, I apologize, but please bear with me and read on to where I justify my contentions. I intend you no malice; on the contrary, I am holding out the hand of human friendship.

"We shouldn't even need the word 'atheism'.
If people didn't invent ridiculous imaginary gods,
rational people wouldn't have to deny them."
Ricky GERVAIS

3. PARABLES AND BELIEF

The first part of Andy's Chapter 2, The Scandinavian Skeptic, is a modern-day parable. It's so good I'm going to quote the beginning of it in full, here is what we might call 'Act One':

"I don't believe that Sweden exists!" my friend suddenly announced from across the coffee-shop table. "There! I've finally said it." He took a long sip of espresso and stared fiercely at me, clearly daring me to respond. I paused for a moment to think, my cinnamon roll halfway to my mouth as I digested what he'd just said.

"Pardon?"

"Sweden doesn't exist. I am a Scandinavian scoffer, a Nordic nullifidian, a Sverigeinian sceptic…"

"And clearly the possessor of quite some thesaurus. But, seriously, you don't believe in Sweden?

"That's right. When you think about it: Sweden is just a political conspiracy, invented to make other European citizens work harder. All that talk of the best healthcare system, the highest standard of living, tall, svelte, and beautiful people. Come on, it sounds more and more like a myth every time you hear it. But I'm not fooled, I don't believe in Sweden."
I stared at my friend silently, allowing the sounds of the coffee shop to drift over us while I pondered. In the background, the radio began playing "Dancing Queen" by ABBA.

"You're insane," I said. "What do you mean you don't believe in Sweden? That's ridiculous. If Sweden doesn't exist,

how do you explain IKEA furniture, or the Swedish chef on The Muppet Show, or what glues Norway to Finland? That's a staggering claim! What's your evidence?"

"Evidence?" my friend asked.

"Yes, evidence. You surely have more than just a hunch and a bunch of prejudices, and must have some pretty impressive evidence for your belief. I realize that Sweden has only 9.5 million inhabitants and more moose than men, but you can't simply deny that it exists."

"Ah," said my friend, knowingly, "I see your problem."

"My problem?"

"Yes, your problem. In fact, your confusion. You think that my denial of Sweden is an actual claim of some kind, that it's a belief. But it isn't. It's a non-belief. There's nothing I need to explain – rather I'm talking about something I lack, namely a belief in Sweden, so I don't need to give any evidence for it."

Doesn't Andy write fiction *well!* I was *there*, in the café, hearing the music, weren't you? He has a novel in him! But, is it a Freudian slip that his example is *Sweden*, a country that is 80% non-believers and has one of the lowest crime rates? In other words, is one of the most moral societies, in the world...

Like the parables of old, Andy's yarn is laced with comfortable familiar references to improve palatability; tags that can easily be mistaken for credibility, or even veracity, by the undiscerning. A good story is sort of *hypnotic* in its ability to convince. We relate strongly to narratives because our very own lives are a sequence of events with a beginning, middle and an end. We can *identify* with a good tale.[16]

Children's author C.S. Lewis once said stories are capable of

'...sneaking past the watchful dragons of the mind',

In other words, stories can *deceive* us. C. S. Lewis was knowingly using his moralizing fairytales to wage a Christian propaganda campaign, and his target audience was *children!* The old genre of fairytale with its *obviously* fantastical child-eating giants (fee, fi, fo, fum), grandma-eating wolves, hateful stepmothers and murderous witches is far less harmful! Just remember, parables (stories) are no substitute for evidence. Neither is poetry – you'd be surprised how many Christians have offered me poetry as evidence for 'god'!

"...no matter how attractive a narrative it is,
it doesn't have any scientific basis..."
Prof Oliver PYBUS, University of Oxford

One story that took hold in Papua New Guinea was that it was respectful to eat the internal organs of one's dead relatives. The tale was told that the deceased's 'spirit' would live on in the consumer and that would help the 'empty' body go to the 'afterlife'. They even fed the tastiest bit of the dead, the brains, to babies. Sadly, this practice brought about an outbreak of the prion disease 'Kuru' that causes holes in the brain and a lingering but early death. It took twenty years from the connection being discovered in the 1960s for the cannibalism of dead relatives to be abandoned, such was the force and influence of the story. What is the value of belief?

In some parts of Africa, albinos, who are born with a genetic condition that prevents their bodies making the melanin that gives skin its color, are murdered by people who believe that their bones contain gold or have 'magical' powers. Witchdoctors claim that amulets made from albino bones can cure disease or bring great wealth to those who wear them. Sometimes a fiction is simply more appealing than the truth. Ask yourself again, what is the value of belief?

Going back to Andy's attempt to enlist the power of storytelling with his 'mythical Sweden' yarn, this reveals common confusions about how and when to best apply the words 'belief', 'disbelief' and 'non-belief'. It's one of many good examples that Andy gives us of how to present a view in the form of a Straw Man Fallacy. In this case the Straw Man's words are spoken by the fictitious 'atheist friend' role being played out in the cafe scenario. How easy it is to put bad arguments into the mouths of 'atheists' *if you write their speech yourself!* Such admirable craftiness!

Andy is trying to show us that it's ridiculous to disbelieve in something as real as Sweden, which is his analogy for 'god'. Analogies are rarely perfect, but this is one of the more ludicrous ones! Nobody makes the claim that Sweden doesn't exist, precisely because it *is* utterly preposterous, so this is a Straw Man Fallacy, a misrepresentation of Andy's opponents' position. Using that comical comparison enables him to make it appear that the silly suggestion that Sweden ('god') doesn't exist *is a claim that requires evidence*. That's an attempt to shift the burden of proof to the denier of Sweden's existence (who would do that?); to try to make us 'prove' a negative, which is known as Russell's Teapot Fallacy[17]. Furthermore, evidential Sweden is *not* analogous to non-evidential 'god' so that is a case of the Fallacy of False Equivalence – three examples of bad reasoning in one! A triple whammy!

Let me explain:

- Sweden is *material*. There is copious evidence for its existence in the form of shareable repeatable observations. So its existence is beyond question and therefore *not* a matter for active belief or disbelief.

- On the other hand, 'god', allegedly, is *'immaterial'*[18]. A hypothetical, non-evidential (up to the present moment), 'immaterial being'. Therefore the claim that She exists *is* open to active belief or disbelief.

Andy is trying to argue that an irrational disbelief in evidential Sweden, which only a fool would express, makes it rational to believe in a non-evidential god!

I am palming my head in amazement at the convoluted contortions of thought that theists have to go through when trying to defend their position!

Now let's take a close look at this paragraph of Andy's:

"You're insane," I said. "What do you mean you don't believe in Sweden? That's ridiculous. If Sweden doesn't exist, how do you explain IKEA furniture, or the Swedish chef on The Muppet Show, or what glues Norway to Finland? That's a staggering claim! What's your evidence?" (My underlining)

Right there, Andy reveals that he recognizes *the value of evidence*; that shows promise! I go into evidence in Chapter 4 but first, what do we mean when we use the word 'belief'? Andy acknowledges *two* types of belief when he writes:

"I think we all instinctively know there is a definite difference between active beliefs and passive beliefs"

Andy is correct about there being a difference between active and passive belief, *but he does not elucidate what that difference is.* I will.

36

It's this: *items of unfalsified evidential information ('knowns') do not require active believing, but claims do.* Bear with me and I will explain over the next few pages...

In the following paragraph, Andy almost reveals a sensible grasp of the modern philosophical usage of 'belief' when he writes (My underlinings):

"The problem is that only beliefs or claims can be true or false. For example, it makes perfect sense to ask whether statements such as 'It is raining today' or 'The Maple Leafs lost the hockey again' are true. Those are claims, they are beliefs, and they have what philosophers call a 'truth value'. They are either true or false. On the other hand, it is utterly meaningless to ask whether the colour blue, a small off-duty Slovakian traffic warden, or Richard Dawkins' left foot is 'true'. That would be a bizarre category error. These things are not claims or beliefs and thus do not possess any kind of 'truth value'. They simply are."

I am *so* pleased that Andy groups 'beliefs' and 'claims' together, although I suspect that the full extent of the implications may have escaped him! He is right: beliefs and claims (sentences that describe beliefs) can be true or false, but *items of evidential information (knowns) simply ARE*.

From that one paragraph in his book, the following deductions can be made:

- 'Belief' and 'claim' can be interchangeable synonyms.
- Beliefs/claims can be *evaluated* for veracity, i.e. they are matters for *opinion*, not items of evidential information.
- Beliefs/claims are propositions and, therefore, must include *false* as a possible evaluation.
- We can *disagree* about beliefs/claims *because* they are just *personal* evaluations – *opinions or choices.*
- There is a category of information that is closer to 'true' than beliefs/claims – these are items, like Sweden, that *cannot* be false and, therefore, indisputably ARE.
- Things that indisputably ARE do not come under the purview of believing since they cannot be seriously challenged or evaluated for veracity or falsehood. Such **'Things that ARE'** (knowns) *do not require active belief.*
- 'Truth' can often be distinguished from falsehood (Ask yourself, "How?" Answer: *By means of evidence*).
- Conversely, the need to believe in a proposition implies it is *not* one of the **'Things That ARE'.**
- Therefore, all beliefs, including Andy's belief in a god, are **merely** opinions about propositions or hypotheses.
- So 'god' is just a claim that Andy (and many others) simply *choose(s)* to believe in *as if it were true.*
- Choosing to believe a claim does not make it true.
- So the existence of a 'god' or gods may be just a *false* belief. It's not definitely a known. Knowns don't *need* believing.

I'm comfortable with all of that. Andy is effectively conceding that beliefs, including beliefs in 'gods', are *not* 'concrete facts' but just hypotheses (claims) that are dubious due to the lack of compelling evidence. They might be true *or false*. He is also accepting that the act of believing is just a matter of personal choice, which means it contributes nothing to the acquisition of *real* information. Beliefs may be things that you know, but what you know isn't necessarily correct, factual or valuable. For many centuries, people knew that the sun went round the Earth. We can know the story of Goldilocks and the Three Bears but it's not useful for forming a worldview. 'Knowledge' is subjectively memorized and does not necessarily correspond to objective evidential information. Knowledge is inside the head, information is outside of it.

Furthermore, by reverse logic, if a statement *requires believing* that very *act* must *cast doubt on its veracity*. Being able to assign a truth-value must mean that we are *not* dealing with a **Thing That IS,** but with a *proposition* (hypothesis, claim or belief). Andy correctly tells us that it's inappropriate to apply the test of truth evaluation to **'Things That ARE'.** His **'passive beliefs'** are *knowns* that are unfalsified and therefore beyond the need for actual believing. On the other hand, as Andy acknowledges, **active beliefs *may be false*.** Therefore, since they are *questionable propositions, just dubious claims,* beliefs are *monumentally* *unimportant*. In my view, Andy has just burst the bubble of *all* faiths! What a shot in the foot!

Naturally, Christians perceive this embarrassing association between belief and doubt so they try to lift their belief out of the depths of dubiety by claiming that it is a 'Justified True Belief'. What do they mean by that? It seems to mean they have unearthed some material that they think justifies continuing to believe in their 'god', despite the yawning deficit of evidence. Amusingly, they sometimes enlist *science* in the effort to confirm their bias! It may include radio-isotope dating of artefacts, archeological investigations of ancient locations and reinterpretations of religious texts, none of which can confirm claimed biblical *events*; they are just distractions. A conjuror would call this tactic 'misdirection'.

The 'Justified True Belief' Warriors in action!

40

To distinguish fact from fiction, we should ask, "does it have evidence" (shareable repeatable observations). If the answer is 'yes' then it's a Thing That IS (a known) and doesn't require active believing. If the answer is 'no' then it's a hypothetical and we can choose whether to believe in it or not. Claiming it's a 'Justified True Belief' is an attempt to smuggle a hypothesis through the evidence test as though it's a Thing That IS. JTB is *not* a credible substitute for evidence.

Of course, it's a free country, so you can believe what you like. It's only a personal choice after all. However, I am *not* comfortable with people wishing to *inflict* their *divisive* and *unimportant* beliefs, or values and principles *derived* from their unimportant beliefs, on *others*. Especially when the others are *children,* and *most especially when they encourage the taking up of arms against those who differ,* which the act of believing in a 'god' seems to compel some to do.

Andy quite rightly says it would be *'a bizarre category error'* to ask if Richard Dawkins left foot is true or false, which means he has recognized that there is a class of things (including Sweden) that are so factual that they do not require active believing. This is a commonly accepted idea. Philosopher Karl Popper described such items of information as 'unfalsified', which is as close as it's possible to get, in reality, to 'true'. I prefer to call such things 'unfalsified evidential information' or 'probable truths'. The Stanford Encyclopedia of Philosophy describes these premises as *"concrete facts, which presumably cannot be false."*[19] Donald Rumsfeld (I'm not a fan of his!) called them the 'known knowns'.[20]

I contend that we are relieved of the task of actively believing in such 'Rumsfeld knowns'. They no longer need believing because they are adopted in practice as 'true' and are banked in the library of our memories on the metaphorical shelf labeled 'Givens' or 'Knowns'. *Thankfully!* Imagine the computing power that our brains would require if we had to continuously reassure ourselves that gravity will stop us from floating away! Envisage the *terrible paranoid fear* of nodding off, ceasing to actively believe in gravity through being unconscious, and having nightmares about being scared of drifting away into space! We wouldn't dare to take forty winks!

And wouldn't life be stressful if it consisted of us having to reiterate our *belief* in thousands of unfalsified evidential facts, *all the time!* Ask yourself, would we wake up each morning with no understanding of the world as a consequence of having spent some hours asleep failing to re-affirm and retain the beliefs we had yesterday?

So, yes, Sweden just *is!* It's *not* a belief (claim), so it's not appropriate to disbelieve it. There is plenty of evidence for Sweden's existence and such a 'concrete fact' cannot be a proposition since propositions must permit the alternative evaluations of true or *false*. That is, propositions (claims, beliefs or hypotheses) are matters for *opinion*, unlike Sweden. But, while Sweden is *not* subject to active belief or disbelief, the existence of 'god' definitely *is*. So, comparing Sweden to 'god' is an example of the Fallacy of False Equivalence. Belief in a 'god' is just a chosen opinion about a claim, about a *hypothesis,* about *the UNknown!*

Unlike Sweden, hypotheses are just assumptions that have not passed testing. The etymology of 'hypothesis' is *Gr., hypo, under, tithenai, to place* – in other words it has a low status. Here are some examples of hypotheses: Extraterrestrial Intelligent Life exists; there are Multiple Universes; there is a Creator Deity and a Loch Ness Monster. The whole point of hypotheses is they are just guesses and we don't know whether they are true or not. So you can believe what you like about them, right up until evidence turns the hypothesis into a conclusion one way or the other. This is more likely to happen to some hypotheses than to others, for example, intelligent aliens are highly probable but 'god' is highly *improbable* (Why? See later). In fact, in the case of the 'god' hypothesis, it has deliberately been made *untestable* by defining Her as 'immaterial'. Ask yourself, "Why has this been done?"

So what have we established so far? That the existence of Sweden, like the Solar System and Richard Dawkins' left foot, is *evidential*, being repeatedly observable by anyone at any time, well, anyone in the vicinity of Richard Dawkins in the case of his left foot, and therefore Sweden is not in doubt. Plentiful evidence shows that Sweden exists so it's a 'concrete fact', which doesn't require active believing.

But there is *no* evidence for the existence of a 'god' yet, so 'god' is just a hypothesis, and belief, non-belief or disbelief are all available for persons choosing an attitude to hold towards 'Him, Her or It'. When active belief or disbelief *is* exercised, it is done so on the basis of personal choice, exactly like making a wager, that is, it's a *subjective choice,* and that's not a good thing to the ears of a scientist.

Ask yourself, as disagreement is rife, why should we think that beliefs deliver truth?

Simply put, claims require active belief; 'knowns' do not. Consequently, the need to make the effort of actively believing something reveals it's merely a claim.

A belief is, at best, a positive choice, although not necessarily the choice of the believer himself! Most of us abdicate the job of choosing a faith to our parents and even governments have endorsed that principle!

A Kurdish acquaintance of mine first discovered that he was a Muslim when he saw what the bureaucrats had written in his passport!

45

It's not just the theocracies that do this: recently I had to fill in a data form for my four-year-old daughter's school. One question asked what her religion was! I wrote, "She's too young to have made an informed decision."[21]

The contrary stance to belief: *disbelief* is a negative choice, but *non-belief* is neither positive nor negative. It's a *failure* to choose, the passive position of waiting to be convinced in one direction or the other. In the absence of evidence either for or against a proposition, a thinking person can occupy the default position of skepticism awaiting evidence. That's non-belief. It would be just as unreasonable to actively *disbelieve* a non-evidential proposition as to actively *believe* it.

Active believers and active disbelievers are *opinionated*. They've made a choice; like deciding whether to put sugar in coffee or not. (The decision-making process may be no more important than that, although the outcome may be deemed to be. Beware of men who are dogmatic about their beliefs.)

Here is an example for clarification:

"My horse won" is a concrete fact, it's evidential – no active believing is required. Believing in that statement is redundant.

"My horse will win" is a positive hypothesis – active *belief* is being applied. The race is not over, so no one really knows whether it is true or false yet: it is a controversial opinion. Belief and disbelief are both available to choose between.

"Maybe your horse will win, maybe not, let's wait and see" is the non-belief option. The speaker can't draw a conclusion from no evidence, so he is choosing not to express an opinion.

"Nah, your horse will never win!" is the negative hypothesis - active *disbelief* is being applied. No one really knows whether it is true or false yet; it is a controversial opinion. Belief and disbelief are both available to choose between.

47

In practice, to access the 'concrete facts' we call them to mind when required. It's like bringing them from the hard drive into the RAM. We do not have to forever consciously work at believing them. They have transcended *beyond* the need for active believing. Belief is redundant in respect to them. They are *unfalsified evidential information.* It's as if we have written them down as 'probable truths' in our heads and made a mental note *not* to go to the effort of actively believing them.

> *"The good thing about science is that it's true whether or not you believe in it."*
>
> Neil de Grasse TYSON

I'm a science teacher (retired now), but I've never had to go about all the time actively believing in The Periodic Table! I've memorized most of it and, when I need it (not often these days!) I simply recall it. Here's another example: the only time we ever bother to think about gravity is when we are fearful that we might fall. Even then, we don't question its *veracity* because we know it's a 'concrete fact' not a matter of opinion. Is anyone dubious about the likely outcome of jumping out of a high window? No! That's because the effect of gravity is universally acknowledged to be real and 'true'[22].

Question: How do you know when you've got a 'concrete fact'?

Answer: When evaluation for veracity has ceased and questioning has disappeared to the extent that it would be unreasonable to hold a different opinion/belief.

Example: Do you wonder whether you will fall if a rope bridge breaks while you are crossing it? Do you question the truth of the effect of the force of gravity on Earth? Do you think it is reasonable to hold a different opinion, e.g. that you might float upwards? If your answers are 'No', then you are probably encountering a 'concrete fact' and you can safely cease actively believing in it. Questioning is unrealistic, but not forbidden or discouraged, *as is often the case in religions*. Re-affirmation is not required, unlike in the case of the 'virgin birth'!

Whether ingenuously or naively, theists seem to mix up unfalsified evidential information with mere propositions and to bundle them together under the general heading of 'Beliefs'. Perhaps this worked alright back in the day when there was little real *evidential* information and all knowledge was actually *just* belief in propositions, but it's the twenty first century now and that old meaning of the word 'belief' has outlived its usefulness. Now we know there is another, *better*, category of information – 'concrete facts'. The Age of Believing is over; we are now in the Age of Unfalsified Evidential Information, of Probable Truths or 'Knowns'.

Age of Belief   Age of Evidence

Over the centuries, the act of believing has been demoted from being the *only* 'source' of knowledge to being just a personal preference about a dubious proposition. One category has been split into two. Gradually, throughout history, many beliefs have been turned into 'concrete facts' and we have banked them and moved on. Other beliefs have been shown to be false and we have abandoned them. A few religious beliefs have yet to achieve either transformation. They remain as merely hypotheses for the time being, but the water of understanding is draining from the cistern of beliefs into the pool of knowns.

We all need to recognize that the very act of believing reveals the inconclusiveness, and hence the valuelessness of the 'god' hypothesis. It's in limbo between 'true' and 'false' and therefore just a matter for opinion. Once we have accepted that, we will all grasp that such rampant uncertainty is a crazy basis for choosing our friends, for fundamentalism, for deciding life or death actions. When that realization has become ubiquitous, and I am hopeful that it will, the world will be a safer, less fractious place.

~~~

Usually, at this point some Christians raise one of three red herrings; they say that:

1. Religions do a lot of good things.
2. Religions are not the only sources of disagreement.
3. There are other ways of knowing things than by means of the scientific method.

51

So, here are my responses:

1. **Good things** - No religion has exclusive ownership of charitable works. In fact, Welfare States, International Organizations like the UN and billionaire benefactors like Bill and Melinda Gates, Mark Zuckerberg and Warren Buffet, together with secular charities like Children in Need, Comic Relief, Live Aid and Sport Relief deliver a huge amount for human well-being, and they do it without an obligation to accept the authority of the self-proclaimed representatives of 'god'. Religions notoriously siphon off much wealth for their own purposes and their charity often comes with compulsory recruitment attached. Have you seen the theists' extravagant buildings? Churches certainly know how to impress people with bling! The Anglican Church is one of the biggest landowners in the UK, see here: http://tinyurl.com/hhz7o2m
Why do you think Robin Hood's ecclesiastical buddy Friar *Tuck* was called that? (He was well fed! "tuck" = food) Check out 'televangelists', The Vatican[23] and 'pastorpreneurs' like Creflo Dollar: the clue is in his name!

2. **Disagreement** - That's true. We disagree on politics, fight over resources, squabble about football teams, etc. But at least those things are *real and necessary*, unlike the supposed 'god'. Wouldn't it be better to have one less

52

reason for conflict? Especially when it's only a *hypothetical* reason. Particularly when it is linked to so *much* conflict.

3. **Other ways of knowing** - *Are there?* Please tell me about them! Do you mean by 'reading the tea-leaves'? Palmistry? Crystal ball gazing?

DIFFERENT WAYS OF KNOWING?

Nonsense   Science

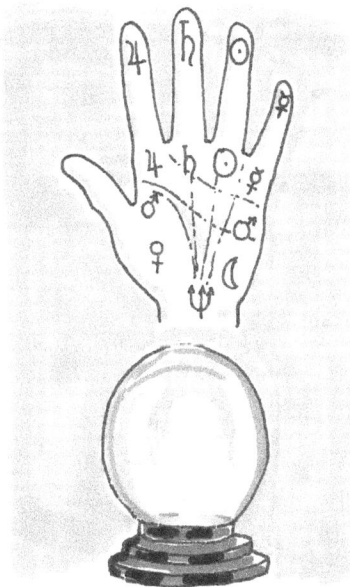

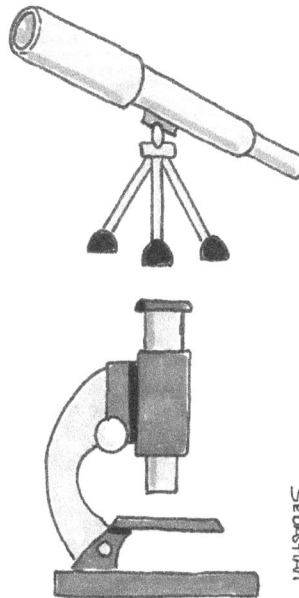

So, we can believe in hypotheses, but belief is not needed for knowns. Once you KNOW, you don't need to believe.

Ask yourself:

Why do religious beliefs need constant reiteration?

Why do believers need to pray daily (or *five times a day*)?

Why do they need services of mass worship every week?

Why do they need to say 'grace' at mealtimes?

Why do they need a calendar of religious events?

Why do life's milestones need *religious* ceremonies?

Why do they need a 'history' recorded in 'scriptures'?

Why do they need bolstering by peer group pressure (including 're-affirming the virgin birth' to each other)?

All of the above activities are perpetrated in the mistaken, but comforting, belief that repetition and a consensus of mass opinion turns a proposition into a truth! That's the Vox Populis Fallacy[24]. It's safety in numbers – it's thinking two billion believers 'can't be wrong'! Well, yes they can! Christians think that one and a half billion Muslims are wrong, don't they? Ask yourself, is devotion to reiteration and a consensus of non-expert opinion a valid way of testing for veracity?

Sadly, the lack of evidence for 'god' forces clergy to attempt to subdue their less gullible flock members with threats of punishment for 'apostasy' (quitting a faith), 'blasphemy' (being rude about 'god') and 'heresy' (disagreeing with church doctrine). Those deemed guilty may receive capital punishment *and* imaginary burning in 'hell' for 'eternity' after death! Such medieval laws and sentences do not curb antisocial acts, or deliver a just and fair society. They are purely for keeping the Christian population under the clerical thumb by means of frightening deterrents for disobedience. It seems that faith leaders are prepared to scare us if we are not willingly submissive. The silk glove of their pretty stories covers an iron fist! There are still some countries[25] in the world where you can be executed for being an 'atheist'. Such barbaric punishments for these bogus 'crimes' are most zealously practised today in the Islamic Theocracies.

The hypothetical nature of belief also explains why, despite the entire communal calendar of events and the programme for commemorating the landmarks of life that is woven into the very fabric of our social existence; despite all the childhood indoctrination; despite the constant reaffirmations of belief in miraculous events; despite the demonization of non-believers; despite the threats of sadistic

punishments for 'crimes' against the religious authority and despite the immense peer pressure to conform, doubt can *still* raise its ugly head *even* in the minds of faith *leaders*.

See here: http://tinyurl.com/nevjacd

and here: http://tinyurl.com/zvqsoln

None of that laborious, yet false, 'confirmatory' process (akin to brain washing) is necessary for *evidential* information; for unfalsified scientific information; for 'concrete facts', because, once established by evidence, 'concrete facts' can be regarded as very probably true, *whether you believe in them or not*. Scientists do not need to meet together and re-affirm their belief in gravity every 'Sabbath'. That's how irrelevant believing is, particularly when belief is *self-affirmed* by presupposition and biased exposure to information; or by biased interpretation of information; or even by the writing of a Christian apologetics book! Such confirmation bias is not an *objective* way of arriving at a conclusion!

OK, yes, before you complain dear reader, the reason why The Stanford Encyclopaedia of Philosophy and I put 'concrete facts' in quotes is because even Unfalsified Evidential Information is not deemed to be *absolutely* certain. This is because open-minded scientists don't like to close the door on the possibility that new observations might cause them to question and revise their models of reality.[26] Unfalsified Evidential Information is a bit like money – we unthinkingly accept that notes and coins have value, right up until the moment that the currency is seriously challenged!

Unless a rare upset, like rabid inflation, devalues the contents of our wallets and purses, we don't have to think about our currency, let alone go about actively believing in it and re-affirming it with our friends. Money is highly probable to be reliable but not utterly absolute.

It's important to realize that all scientific explanations are *provisional*. That should not be a surprise; after all, they are only *conceptual models*. Scientists are open to revise their understanding of reality when new evidence is discovered. Nothing is set in the stone of certainty. We should only use the words 'truth' and 'proof' in a conceptual context because those absolutes have not been found in the cosmos. I try to remember to put the words 'proof' and 'truth' in speech marks (unless already in a quote, of course).

However, there is a vast degree of difference between the scientific situation of evidential conclusions that are *yet to be falsified* (sometimes after hundreds of years of successfully modelling reality) on the one hand, and the 'god' proposition state of affairs of *completely lacking in evidence up to now* on the other. So this lack of *absolute* certainty[27] really shouldn't be used by Christians wishing to impugn that science is as ill-founded as their religion. That would be a Tu Quoque Fallacy anyway and would prove nothing. We call that 'home team refereeing' – treating your side more leniently than the opponents. It's another instance of theists having to resort to attacking the 'opposition' because they have no evidence to support the Christian claim.

Ironically, it's the open-minded scientists, the constructors of so many evidential theories that successfully model reality, who modestly retain a modicum of doubt. While those with zero evidence for their claims (believers) are the ones who close-mindedly and dogmatically assert *utterly certain knowledge* from their pulpits! Such nonsense!

So here's the *real* situation: ordinary dictionaries have got it wrong with their out-of-date definition of belief, which is typically, *'a proposition that is held to be true'*. Nowadays we understand that beliefs are just personally chosen attitudes towards propositions; claims that can be *false*; claims that can

58

be *challenged and argued against;* merely *matters of opinion.* Andy's example of Sweden, is *not* a matter of opinion – it's a known, whereas 'god', being 'immaterial' (allegedly), *is* just a claim or proposition because Her existence currently lacks evidence. It's an analogy that actually works the *opposite* way to how Andy would like it, by highlighting the *real tangible difference* between Sweden and 'god'!

In fact, 'god' being 'immaterial' is a big problem for believers because at the moment we have no means of investigating the 'immaterial', so there is no chance of gathering any evidence for Her right now. This means She is doomed to remain merely a hypothesis until 'immaterial' detection technology is developed, and we have no idea how to do that!

Furthermore, when, or if, 'god' is discovered, She will have to be instantly reclassified as material, i.e. real! 'God' would suddenly cease to be supernatural and would presumably lose all of Her alleged super powers! Would you want such a mundane, *normal* 'god'? Or is it best for you that 'god' remains safely evidence-free? As just a glorified wish...

So, being just a proposition, 'god' is a suitable subject for opinion, for belief or disbelief, unlike Sweden. Belief is tailor-made for dubious claims such as, "There is a god". It's this very uncertainty about 'god's' existence and nature that makes it possible for there to be so many different, incompatible, 'god-based' religions *and* it's why it's legitimate to be a doubter. Contrast the weakness of the claims of 'god' with the Unfalsified Evidential Information about gravity...

Ask yourself, can it be that this *very need* for continuous reiteration of active belief actually reveals the truly *hypothetical* nature of the 'god' proposition? After all, we know that the supporters of other faiths are just expressing a mistaken opinion, don't we? Isn't it our opinion that *their* beliefs are *not* 'true'? Isn't that why we don't share *their* beliefs? Isn't that why we don't attend *their* place of worship? Of course, *they* hold the same dubious opinion about the veracity of *our* beliefs. Since we are all 'others' in respect to each other, why can we not see the near valuelessness of *all* opinions and beliefs? Come to think of it, what's the difference between a belief and an opinion[28]?

Religions promote division and alienation. Ask yourself, does it make sense to divide mankind into factions based on personal predilections for worshipping different *non-evidential hypothetical* deities? Should inevitably dubious beliefs be grounds for making political decisions, *like whether to attack?*

Of course, Andy Bannister *imagines* (believes) that his belief is important. That's why he assumes that 'atheism' must be an important belief for me too. It's why he finds it hard to envisage that 'atheists' are not consumed by a similar devotion to an ideology.

Andy gets into such a contortion trying to make out that 'atheism' is a positive belief. He even claims that Richard Dawkins must be motivated by 'atheism' to write books and go on speaking tours. See the following quote from The Atheist Who Didn't Exist:

"What was it that drove him (Richard Dawkins) *to pour endless hours into typing, drafting, editing and refining? Presumably it was his atheism."* (My bracket.)

This is yet another example of the Mind Projection Fallacy: imagining that the attitudes and behaviours of others have the same motivation as your own. In other words, because Andy himself writes books and goes on speaking tours *inspired by his beliefs*, he thinks a theistic type of ideology like his must activate us all. Why do theists think that 'atheism' has any doctrine to disseminate? Ask yourself, why would anyone work on behalf of *no* god? Do theists think the same of 'afairyism' and 'afairyists'? If not, why not?

It's true that a belief can be a guiding force in the service of a divisive cause, and it's time for me to make a confession: I've felt that force! There was a decade in my life when I walked the streets feeling virtuous, convinced in the righteousness of my actions, believing that what I was up to was beneficial to local residents! However, in my case, the guiding force was politics! I'd been elected as Leader of the Opposition in a large Council and I believed I was working to save the people from the tyrannically uncaring policies of the ruling party! That was many years ago. I'm no longer politically active.

Here's the thing, Richard Dawkins and I are *science educators*. Teaching Science is different from teaching one of the humanities. Subjects like English, Maths, Geography, History, RE and Languages are largely about imparting a body of information but Science, although it includes imparting some facts, involves training students in a *style of thinking*. Science teachers are motivated by the desire to help people to know how to think for themselves. To help them learn how to construct an investigation; how to be skeptical; to scrutinize; criticize and to recognize evidence. What we are

62

doing is trying to alert people to the perils likely to befall them if they don't develop rational thinking ability. It would be unprofessional, perhaps immoral, for a science teacher to do otherwise and leave people open to deception.

Richard Dawkins was the University of Oxford's Professor for Public Understanding of Science from 1995 until 2008. Teaching Science is our positive incentive, our mission, not 'atheism'. If we could invent Rationalin^{TM}, a pill to make people think clearly, we would. It would save us a lot of work! Until then, we can only present Unfalsified Evidential Information and explain how to obtain it; either way we have no power over what people *choose to believe...* You can believe sugar improves coffee if you wish... That's the level of significance belief should have.

Interestingly, if evidence *was* forthcoming for the 'god' hypothesis, it might tip it over into the state of a 'concrete fact', just like gravity and then, like gravity, 'god' would cease to be a consideration for active belief or disbelief. Evidence would transform 'god' from a proposition into a conclusion for which active belief would be needless. Ironic or what?

The fact is, many thousands of years of human endeavor have failed to achieve the conversion of even one 'god' from a belief into a 'concrete fact'. On the contrary, history is littered with the stories, images and icons of thousands of 'gods' that are now acknowledged to have been fictitious and that have died out through the loss of their believers. Yet people *still* look at their own 'god' and think, "She is the only *true* one."

64

You might complain, dear reader, that this idealistic polarizing of information into just two classes: *'concrete facts'* and *hypotheses*, with little or no middle ground, is unreasonable. You might ask how do we select which of the two categories to put newly encountered information into? Well, obviously, it depends on the source of the information – new ideas are just concepts but new repeatable observations are facts that can turn concepts into conclusions. Repeatability is not just doing the same investigation again tomorrow, it *can* mean observations being made at different times, but it can also mean simultaneous observations from different locations or by using different means of detection.

What about the items that are not yet 'concrete facts' but seem to be making progress in that direction? The things that are at the frontiers of investigation... Well, right up until repeatable observations show a proposition to be correct or incorrect, it should be regarded as a hypothesis and, at the moment of discovery of such evidence, it should be considered to have suddenly flipped over into a conclusion. Any notion that is still under investigation remains hypothetical. It's rather like the refraction of light as it passes into a different medium. There is no intermediate bending stage; the beam suddenly angles at the boundary.

Of course, our upbringing may have a big effect on our attitudes towards new propositions. We have either been raised to be skeptical or gullible, and each of us will make our own judgment based on what we consider to be worthy as evidence (see next chapter). Theists understand the permanence of ideas instilled in childhood, that's why they insist on Christenings, Baptisms, Sunday school attendance, Worship in school assemblies, etc. It's why the Jesuits have a saying: "Give me a boy at seven and I'll show you the man."

Where are you on the Scale of Readiness to Believe?

Properly Skeptical   Persuadable   Really Gullible

←----|--------------|------------------------------------|-----------------→

'Concrete Facts'   Plausible Stories   Mere Hypotheses

Evidence   Parables and Poetry

The following table might help you to choose which way to go:

'BELIEFS'	'KNOWNS'
'Supported' by Argument, Parables and 'Faith' Conceived Subjectively	Supported by Evidence (Repeatable Observations) Discovered Objectively
Untestable Dubious Hypotheses	Tested and Highly Probable to be Accurate Models of Reality
Often Intended to be Unfalsifiable	Unfalsified
Believing essential (yet beliefs of others doubted!)	Active Believing is NOT Required
Culturally Determined or Personally Chosen	Accepted by Consensus of Experts, then by public
Need Constant Re-affirmation	Notionally under permanent Review
Claimed to be 'Certain'	Acknowledged to be Provisional
Specifically Belong to the Believers	Freely Available in the Public Domain
Questioning is Discouraged	Questioning is Encouraged

Most of the time though, we don't examine the evidence for an item of information at all. We just take it on trust or by 'gut feeling', and this is where childhood input might have the biggest impact. If we've been taught scientific method and have learned how to think critically and skeptically, we might trust empirical data more readily than other sources. But if we've been forced to attend church regularly in childhood or made to memorize ancient religious texts by rote chanting, then scriptural stories might be all we know of as 'true'. If we've had neither training then *any* claim might seem plausible to us. Such people are vulnerable to deception. Lead me to 'em! Psst! Wanna buy London Bridge?

Proselytizers and theocratic rulers love an ignorant society, that's why the following are the case:

- Boko Haram means 'Western education is forbidden'.
- The Islamic fundamentalists of Pakistan don't educate girls (Nobel prize winner Malala Yousafzai[29] was shot in the face on her way to school, aged 11) and boys only get taught to recite the Qur'an.
- Illegal Jewish schools that teach the Talmud, but not English and Math, have been discovered in London.

Education, especially scientific education, is as much the recognized enemy of all faiths as it is the benevolent weapon of antitheists.

Until evidence for 'god' arrives, 'god' hypotheses (beliefs) can be strongly held or weakly held. You can be a strong believer in your chosen 'god' hypothesis (fundamentalist) or a weak believer (moderate), but there can only be one level of non-belief, since that is situated at zero. Being a null position, non-belief requires no supporting evidence.

Beware of fundamentalists and be cautious of moderates. Moderates may seem harmless but they may close their eyes to atrocities being done by their religion's extremists and they usually raise their children in the faith so they may be unwilling or unwitting parents of future fundamentalists...

However, active *disbelieving* in 'god' is a dogmatic stance that *does* require an attempt at justification. This will probably fail since negative evidence requires the elimination of all possible traces from the entire realm or domain in which the 'god' is claimed to exist. "There are no cookies in this jar" *is* verifiable but, in the case of the universe, that degree of exclusion is not possible. The universe is just too big. My advice: don't claim 'there is no god' – it's indefensible.

So, for instance, the anthropogenic climate change deniers are expected to produce information to provide support for their position. In such cases, evidence *may* be forthcoming, but no-one can disprove the hypothesis that there is an 'immaterial creator deity' lurking somewhere within, or even 'outside', the unimaginably vast universe any more than they can disprove the existence of the 'immaterial' hippo that I claim occupies my bathroom.

That's the big advantage to 'immateriality' – no one can refute your claims! Of course, making a proposition immune to falsifiability means it is *unscientific*. Andy Bannister himself acknowledges the silliness of the 'immaterial' bathroom Hippo proposition (it was his idea in The Atheist Who Didn't Exist). *Why doesn't he apply the same reasoning to an 'immaterial god'?*

So, some believers claim that their creator deity is 'immaterial' and that She resides in a 'heavenly[30]' 'supernatural[31]' realm to which we may 'transcend[32]' if we are 'righteous[33]' to enjoy an 'afterlife[34]' of eternal bliss! Ask yourself, does that sound like a cunning system designed to prevent Her being 'disproved'?

Amazingly, that collection of *non-evidential concepts* has been so deeply woven into our culture that believers mistakenly think they can demand that I should demonstrate that their 'god' *doesn't* exist! I wonder if that's their general policy – to believe every claim, every Tinker Bell, Humpty Dumpty and Goldilocks, until it's *'disproven'*? It would be a very strange and vulnerable way of living! People would be lining up to sell them London Bridge!

'Prove' and 'disprove' belong in the Conceptual Realm. Scientists would use 'falsified', but please notice it's only the *Christian* 'god' that they challenge me to 'disprove'. They don't ask me to 'disprove' Ganesha or Shiva! Do they consider other people's 'gods' to have *already* been 'disproven'? Why? I suspect this might be another example of 'home team refereeing'! Ask them to 'disprove' Zeus and see how they do it. Then use that method to 'disprove' their 'god'!

Such Contrary Cognition benefits from being instilled in childhood so that the doctrines can be trotted out like Nursery

Rhymes or Multiplication Tables. In Western society today it comes from the unjustified but traditional ubiquity of Christian-style thinking and language, Christian sponsorship of education, Christian easy access to the media, Christian involvement in life events and state ceremonial, etc. All of which, until recently, had become accepted as the norm in the West with 'atheism' being viewed as an abnormality. An Archbishop can get airtime much easier than me!

Throughout history men have believed all sorts of things that we now know are incorrect – iron ships will sink, heavier than air machines will not fly, the heart is the 'seat' of the emotions, heavy stones will fall faster than light ones of the same dimensions. We have succeeded in shaking off all those wrong ideas but Christianity inexplicably survives.

Now I know I'm going to be accused of 'Scientism'[35] because it's happened to me before, but that accusation is just another example of theistic thinking. Believers' failure to find any ideology in 'atheism' itself leads them to try to conflate it with other 'isms' like scientism, materialism and naturalism, which are also *not* ideologies either but they ignore that! On pages 23/24 we saw how Christians try to ally 'atheism' with the real ideology of Communism. These are all just attempts to make out that 'atheism' is a heinous doctrine. Ask yourself, doesn't the theists' need to link 'atheism' with other 'isms' reveal the weakness of their claim that 'atheism' *itself* is an ideology?

'Scientism' is just another fabricated attempt to paint non-believers as rival ideologues who can be attacked on the same playing field as believers. As they do this, oddly, other believers are attempting to bask in the credibility of science! They call themselves by sciencey sounding names: Christian Scientists, Creation Research Institute, Scientology, etc. Make up your minds – is science good or bad?

Unfortunately for the would-be science denigrators, there are *no* scientific doctrines. This is just another example of the Straw Man tactic commonly used by theists to 'justify' their stance. No Head of Research issues an edict that everyone should have Einstein's mad hairstyle and wear a lab-coat everywhere they go, but specifying a dress code and beard style is exactly what some religious leaders do!

Indeed the very opposite is true: science transcends culture and fosters a questioning and open community where different views are listened to; that's often how new discoveries are made. The acceptance of Einstein's Theory of Relativity is an example of the willingness of scientists to change their attitudes. There is no ideology of science; nothing is carved in stone. 'Scientism', like 'atheist', 'heathen' and 'infidel', is a term used by believers to *demonize* people who don't believe in *their* 'god'. How would they like it if I invented a word? Here you are: 'Faithism': a psychological condition brought on by an overzealous belief in a 'god'!

Scientists do *not* meet up and decide what behaviors to impose on society. It's *religions* that enforce conformity. They have to: how else would Christians be able to target their recruitment mission onto the people *without* the crosses or fish symbols? Much time would be wasted trying to convert the already converted!

The truth is that science is the only successful method for discovering information so there's no challenger, no alternative choice. Scientific method is the sensible way to go because of the overwhelming evidence of its success; it reveals 'knowns' that *don't require belief* so it's not a belief system called 'scientism'.

Here is the dictionary meaning of 'ideology': *an ideology is a set of opinions or beliefs of a group or an individual. Very often ideology refers to a set of political beliefs or a set of ideas that characterize a particular culture. So,* Marxism *is* an ideology but neither 'atheism' nor 'scientism' are ideologies because there is no *'set of opinions or beliefs'* associated with them. 'Atheism' is merely a doubtful attitude to a single claim; calling it an ideology is just a mechanism to enable theists to denigrate non-believers and to feel secure in their lack of evidence for a 'god'. Science is just a method of investigation.

Do you believe in any of the following: Nessie, Goblins, Gnomes, Leprechauns, Ghosts, Fairies, Unicorns, Centaurs, Pegasus? No? Does the absence of belief mean that these things are ideologies and must have an 'ism' suffix (Leprechaunism) or an antonym with an 'a' prefix (Agnomist)?

Later in The Atheist Who Doesn't Exist, Andy introduces the 'Brain in a Vat[36]' proposition, he says:

But it's nevertheless possible that you could be mistaken, deceived, or deluded, or that you might actually be just a brain in a jar, wired up to electrodes, stimulated by a mad scientist who is simply manipulating you to conceive of the ice-cream.

Yes, of course, anyone, including Andy and I, might be mistaken, deceived or deluded, but the 'Brain in a Jar' challenge is a desperate attempt to question *all* scientific understanding until you remember that our brains are immensely capable and can fabricate unreal ideas. The impossible drawings of M C Escher[37] and others illustrate this ability well. This capacity for inventing unreal notions occurs in what I call 'The Conceptual Realm' of the 'software' (the 'mind') of the brain. You can conceive of a design for a house but it will remain in the conceptual realm until you have built it, at which point it will become repeatedly observable because it will exist in the Natural Realm. Unlike that house, the 'Brain in a Jar' notion is a non-evidential, untestable concept and therefore of no use.

Mathematics, logic, language, unmade inventions and artistic ideas are all conceptual. Logic is a function of the human brain; we have evolved to identify patterns, to try to understand our environment. It's an aptitude that confers survival, which increases breeding opportunities so that our most advantageous characteristics, which include our behavioral abilities, get passed on.

Some people mistakenly conclude that, since the rules of logic cannot be deviated from, those rules must objectively exist. They are making a category error. The way in which our minds use language for thinking explains why some make this mistake; they incorrectly deduce that the words we use to describe systems or functions actually exist. This leads them to mistake a model of reality for reality itself. Chess has rules and we know they are conceptual. Logic has rules too but, for some strange reason, theists don't want to accept that they are also conceptual. ALL rules are conceptual, fabricated, some correspond to reality and some don't.

Logic provides the rules for the most *rigorous* type of thinking, but it's still *only* thinking. Thinking is conceptual; it enables us to create models in our minds but it remains necessary to test these concepts in order to discover if they match observations or not. When you have arrived at an outcome from your philosophical deliberations you haven't finished, you haven't discovered anything. You have only come to the end of conceptualising. That's the beginning of investigating. The only way of verifying concepts is by testing for a match with nature. Don't mistake the concept of 'trees' for real trees!

Our brilliantly imaginative brains have given us some pretty wild concepts – Phlogiston, Lamarckism, Mohammad riding to Paradise on a winged horse, Jesus walking on water, Moses cleaving the Red Sea, Resurrection, Reincarnation, Unicorns, Dragons, Daleks, Humpty Dumpty, Afterlife, and there will continue to be many more creative concepts – String Theory? Multiversity? The Supernatural? The Superdupernatural? Why stop there? Incidentally, falsification doesn't stop conceptualization – we can still *think* of Humpty Dumpty.

Thinking, including the philosophical style of thinking, knows no limits – we often call imaginative wishful ideas 'dreams'. That's why thoughts have to be tested to see if they match observations. But neither the 'Immaterial' concept nor the 'Brain in a Vat' idea *can* be tested. They are cul-de-sac notions, untestable assumptions. Being untestable is no basis for thinking that they are real; but it *does* mean they are *unscientific*...

Bertrand Russell pointed out that, although there is no way to prove that reality is not just a dream (it is logically possible that you are dreaming now as you read these words on the page or screen), there is no reason why this *should* be the case. So much for logic! *'Logically plausible' does NOT mean 'proven to be true'!* Recently, I asked Anil Seth, Professor of Cognitive & Computational Neuroscience at Sussex University, whether he knew he was not a Brain in a Vat. He said, *"No, but it's my best guess!"* So I contend that it's not useful to postulate that you are a Brain in a Vat but it *is* useful to recognize that you *are* a brain in a cranium.

Every now and then philosophical thinking produces an outcome that, upon testing, *does* usefully model reality. This explains the value of logic and maths. These are important conceptual tools, like language, that can often give a good descriptive match for the phenomena we actually observe. Interestingly, theists sometimes challenge my assessment of what is in the conceptual realm on the grounds that, according to them, maths is *real,* not conceptual, because geometrical patterns exist in all sorts of natural structures. This leads them to imagine that maths is discovered not invented. That is another example of mistaking a model of reality for reality itself. Can they deny that zero and infinity are both mental fabrications and that there is no character for three in binary? I doubt it! The fact is, sometimes a new maths concept is invented *before* the discovery of its observation in reality and sometimes *afterwards*. (More about all this in Chapter 9)

But if you ask them whether *words* are real, not conceptual, some will accuse you of being silly! Strangely, these people can understand that you need a brain to conceive of *words* but they can't grasp that the same applies to *numbers!* In fact both words and numbers are useful fabrications that can *represent* reality in a similar way to how a two dimensional drawing can depict a three dimensional view. The representation can be convincing but a simple test, like poking a finger at the illustration, will expose it as unreal. Patterns *can* be real but recognising them, naming them and representing them is conceptual. Remember, Sir Isaac Newton invented calculus and Napier invented logarithms – *they weren't discovered under a stone!* In our digital age, new algorithms are being invented every day. I expect one day soon they will be assembled into an artificial brain...

Early in human history we had no means of sorting the philosophical wheat from the philosophical chaff, but *now* we do. We have Scientific Method(s)[38] involving testing for evidence. Thanks to the combination of rigorous thinking (philosophy) and investigating for evidence (science), we have been able to achieve some wonderful feats. For instance, I'm immensely proud to be a member of the species that created the Rosetta spacecraft and its lander, Philae.[39]

The philosophical style of thinking is useful for conceiving hypotheses and devising scientific investigation methods but it is observations that enable us to conclude which hypotheses model reality and which are the fanciful ones; it's a perfect partnership. It's like distinguishing between the representational art of the great portrait or landscape painters and the unrealistic art of the surrealists and impressionists. They are both art (concepts in this analogy) but one attempts to model observations while the other is stuck in the imagination, and comparison against reality (repeatable observations in this analogy) enables us to recognize which is which: one matches observations, the other doesn't.

The 'god' concept has achieved the hypothesis stage (She has been conceptualised), but not the conclusion stage. We are waiting for observational evidence. We have been waiting for millennia...

Now, I know some theists will accuse me of trying to use philosophy to disprove philosophy itself, which would be a circular argument, but I contend that I'm not attempting to *disprove* philosophy. I'm merely trying to point out that it is just *thought* to those who mistakenly elevate it to the level of fact. I can see no other way to do that than by comparing it to information that has been derived from external observations.

Sometimes theists complain that my regarding thought as conceptual is my 'philosophy' and then I have to point to the enormous success that scientific method has enabled. There is an obvious difference between thought alone and thoughts that have been grounded in observations. Occasionally I get accused of 'contradicting' myself by using language, which is necessarily conceptual and therefore, according to them, I can't logically believe what I'm contending! Well, I'm not sure how they expect me to convey my position if I'm not allowed to use language! Earlier in this chapter we saw that my belief, or yours, is unimportant. What matters is whether a proposition has an accurate match to observed reality or not. Once a match has been established, belief becomes redundant.

Some theists take their reasoning to ridiculous lengths and claim, "*You* are evidence for 'god'!" It's obviously wishful thinking. How do you make the leap from Her to me? There is no connection, so it's a Non Sequitur Fallacy. Were scientifically eradicated diseases polio[40], smallpox[41] and rinderpest[42] evidence for 'god' too? She didn't take much care of them did She, permitting us to exterminate them the way we did! What about all the extinct species (99.9% of all the species that have ever existed), were they evidence for 'god' too? She was pretty careless with them as well! If my existence is evidence for the Christian 'god', it must be evidence for Zeus too! And, surely, extinct species must be much weightier evidence *against* Her existence! Such nonsense.

The next tactic theists try in their hopeless quest, is to challenge reality. They say we only fabricate a perception of reality in our brains. There is some legitimacy in that, because we all live in an approximate representation of reality that takes our brains about a third of a second to construct out of the signals from our assorted sense organs (some of which arrive at the brain fractionally later than others). But take the game of baseball for example: you can pitch the ball at me, I can accidentally bat it up in the air and a fielder can run underneath and catch it. How is that supposed to work if reality is not real? Our perception may be fabricated from a mix of incoming information and past experience of how the world works, but we obviously construct a pretty accurate representation that is definitely *shared by the other players*.

So this *perceived reality* is *not* purely subjective. It's based on objective data provided by our sense organs to which the brain has added some detail from its memory banks. It's generally good enough, but we can be fooled by optical illusions for example, and it can be defeated by speed; we've all been hit by something that arrived too fast for us to process avoidance.

Challenging reality poses a serious problem for believers because they claim to have access to the 'truth' from their 'god'. 'Truth' has been defined, since the time of Aristotle, as 'corresponding to reality', so theists risk pulling the rug from under their own feet! If reality is unreal then truth must be uncertain and they don't want to admit that! Alternatively, reality must be *incomplete* if their claim of a 'supernatural' realm is correct! To avoid this problem, some prefer 'immaterial' to 'supernatural' and claim that 'immaterial' is real but undetectable! Whichever wriggle they attempt, pointing to scientific ignorance and disregarding the vast amount of information that scientists have discovered shows how desperate theists are to defend their non-evidential propositions. How they must wish for some cold hard facts...

Now look at this example of Dr Andy Bannister's 'logic':

The first problem is that the statement "Atheism is just non-belief in God" proves too much. What do I mean? Well, if this claim is true, consider what it entails. It would mean, for instance, that my cat is an atheist, because she does not believe in God. Likewise, potatoes, the colour green, Richard Dawkin's left foot and small rocks are all atheists because they, too, do not possess a deity of any kind.

In his attempt to prove that 'atheism' is a belief rather than a lack of belief, Andy protests that since a small rock doesn't believe in 'god' it must be an atheist! He's not deducing that brainless things lack the capacity for belief, which *would* make sense, *but that they hold the WRONG belief!*

Once again, Andy thinks he knows how 'atheists' think better than 'we' do! He wouldn't want to associate brainlessness with belief would he, that would insult believers! 'Therefore' he claims 'atheism' is not a negative condition but a positive one! Would he question his own disbelief in the Tooth Fairy on the grounds that a potato must be an Afairyist? Would not believing in fairies also *'prove too much'* in Andy's mind? Ask yourself, is he desperately clinging to a presupposition that is rapidly going down the drain?

This is the curious way you have think if you imagine that 'atheism' is a belief system that can be adopted! Is Andy's cat an 'afairyist' as well? Andy seems to be offering the concept of his cat as an 'atheist' to illustrate what he considers to be a bad argument. He's trying to ridicule 'atheism' by making out

84

that it's foolish for 'atheists' to entertain the possibility that cats might also be 'atheists'! It's another Straw Man Fallacy. Ask yourself, is it wise for anyone to claim to know how cats think? Remember Andy's earlier attempt to ridicule 'atheists'? This one: *Andy is trying to argue that irrational disbelief in an evidential Sweden makes it rational to believe in a non-evidential god!* The 'cat atheist' is another example of this bizarre style of thinking.

Andy has probably been raised on a diet of Genesis 1:26:

Then God said, "Let Us make man in Our image, according to Our likeness; and let them rule over the fish of the sea and over the birds of the sky and over the cattle and over all the earth, and over every creeping thing that creeps on the earth."

The Bible is full of arrant nonsense like that, unsurprisingly, since it was written in an age of profound ignorance. Nobody knows what 'god' looks like so how can we be 'made in Her image'? Are the sufferers from genetic diseases also made in Her image? Are deformed still-born babies made in Her image? Is She a man? Who knows?

Of course, it's very possible to do it the other way round – to invent a 'god' who looks like us! That has been done many times in the past – Anubis is an ancient Egyptian 'god' with a human body and a dog's head, Nu Gua is a human headed

Chinese snake god. They are both discredited 'gods' who no longer attract believers. Ask yourself, why is that? Is it because there is no evidence that they are real?

Cats being 'atheists' may look like a foolish claim from the point of view of a Christian steeped in the egocentric Biblical supposition that the universe was made just for us and that there is a large discontinuity between man and 'the animals'. But DNA evidence shows that no such gulf exists and the universe was around for billions of years before humans arrived on the scene, so those claims are just ridiculous. In fact, there is a broad continuum of increasing complexity and sophistication through the, badly named, 'Tree of Life' ('Bush of Life' would be better).

Chimpanzees, elephants and dolphins are examples of animals that show self-awareness – we know they have a theory of mind because they can trick each other, show guilt, grief and forgiveness or co-operate in play, see here: http://tinyurl.com/q8q9y28 Therefore, although we don't actually *know*, the possibility of 'cat beliefs' remains firmly on the table. Like us, kittens are born *without* any beliefs but, unlike us, they don't appear to understand much speech so they are *not* vulnerable to indoctrination by parents, pastors, priests, mullahs or rabbis (whichever gets to us first!) so the real question is, 'Can a cat be a theist?' Surely, if they can't be inducted into a religion, which seems likely to be the case, cats must retain their natural-born lack of belief throughout life, mustn't they?

DO KITTENS GET INDUCTED INTO A FAITH?

Cats are able to make choices, as cat-owners who have seen them refuse food will well know, so the important question is whether they can form abstract concepts or not. They have the first requirement for believing: a brain, but we don't know yet whether cats' brains are capable of pondering existential questions and constructing beliefs. So, Andy's cat may, or may not, be an 'atheist'. Ask yourself, how could we tell?

The fact is that our relationship with cats over the millennia has resulted in an evolution of their behavior (yes, behaviors, and hence moralities, can evolve). They have learned that they don't have to become snarling adults hunting for prey. In the domestic environment they now retain their kittenish personality throughout life. Biologists call this retention of juvenile behavior, 'Infantilism'. It's a role that suits humans looking for a pet to care for. From the cat's point of view then, a cat owner is a god-like provider and protector. Domestic cats have learned that if they play cute they can enjoy a highly desirable life of idleness and luxury. Is that a belief of theirs? It's certainly a passport to a 'Feline Heaven on Earth' and so, to pussy, *Andy may very well be a worship-worthy 'god'!*

SEbAstiAn

Could it be that inventing a 'loving father in the sky' is a human attempt at *self*-infantilization? Have we been compelled, by the scariness of real life, *to invent a compassionate owner for ourselves in the role of 'His' pets?*

This is yet another example of Andy's backwards thinking technique derived from his mistaken notion that non-belief is an ideology. As usual, his statement contains an assumption – that 'atheism' is an institution, something you can belong to or join. It's the very opposite of that, 'atheists' are a motley non-collection of non-joiners. I expect that Andy is an Afairyist, along with a massive majority of the enormously diverse human population, including me. We have never met at any Afairyist meeting. Is it because not believing in fairies is a non-belief rather than a shared belief? Spot a parallel anyone?

Not content with his *'my cat's an atheist'* thought, Andy pushes the envelope even further with this convoluted idea:

Likewise potatoes, the color green, Richard Dawkins' left foot, and small rocks are all atheists because they, too, do not possess a belief in a deity of any kind! (My exclamation mark)

Despite his attempt to include them, vegetables, colors, Richard Dawkins' body parts and lumps of rock (Andy is using the Fallacies of False Equivalence and False Dilemma again here) cannot be believers *or* disbelievers since they lack the necessary equipment (a brain) for having any attitude towards any proposition. Thinking otherwise is just silly, which is how Andy wishes to make 'atheists' look. Does anyone really think we have to make a case for potatoes not having beliefs?

ATHEISTS! (Do they also disbelieve in the Tooth Fairy?)

Once again, it's obvious that Andy, in the face of no evidence *for* his 'god' belief, is reduced to arguing *against* what he imagines to be the opposite position – ridiculing non-belief. He creates another Straw Man encounter with an 'atheist' just to demonstrate how he would handle it. He thinks he has the answer when his self-penned female 'atheist' friend protests, *"But a potato can't believe anything!"* Here's his response:

"So you're now saying that atheism is the lack of belief in God by a creature that has the ability to form beliefs?"

Well, yes, we are! Furthermore, it's surprising that Andy has even asked that question! I can't say I've noticed him at the greengrocer's preaching to potatoes in the hope of converting them to Christianity, so I assume it must be a rhetorical question. But to make out that the need for a brain turns an absence of belief into a positive claim is just silly.

Andy goes on:

You see that is a different claim entirely. Why? Because it's a positive claim. My atheist friend is now claiming that the external world really exists, that we are not simply brains in a jar, our thoughts and experiences manipulated like those of the humans in The Matrix movies. Furthermore, she is claiming that other minds exist, that it is possible for the human brain to form beliefs, and that our thinking is more or less reliable.

90

Really? Those claims are only made by people of an *'atheistic' persuasion,* are they*?* How so? Hasn't Andy just described the background against which we must *all,* including himself, make our decisions and choose our beliefs? Where do Christians live if not in the natural world with the rest of us? Does he really doubt that other minds exist? Even some animals have a Theory of Mind[43]. Ask yourself, how do those patently normal and natural conditions turn *not* believing in a 'god' into a *positive claim?*

This weird style of thinking makes me wonder whether a list of All The Inanimate Objects That Lack Sight would be a coherent positive category in Andy's mind! Don't these kind of statements include a *negative* concept – 'absence', 'lack', 'not', or the prefix 'a' meaning 'without'? You can't manipulate that into a 'positive' by writing a convoluted parable around it. If that were possible, negativity could be completely eliminated! It seems to me that the mental toolbox of theists has the 'god' spanner in the top tray so the first wrench they reach for is a misfit for the nuts and bolts of nature...

Of course, not *all* information is dubious. Do you doubt you will fall if you leap off a cliff? Do we have to keep re-affirming to ourselves that we will get burnt if we put our fingers in a flame? One experience is enough for most of us isn't it? So, does that type of undisputed information require belief? No! Unfalsified evidential information transcends the need for active believing. We bank it as 'known'. Therefore the appropriate way to use the word 'belief' is in relation to *dubious* propositions, mere hypotheses, e.g. "I believe my horse will win."

CLAIMS	KNOWNS

BELIEF NEEDED	**BELIEF NOT NEEDED**

Once you *KNOW*, you don't need to believe.

STRAW MEN

Theists often ask me questions like these:

"How does your not knowing about how life began to exist negate the existence of creator?"

    It doesn't.

"What is your evidence that a creator doesn't exist?"

    I don't have any

    Do you have any evidence that fairies don't exist?

Here's how it works:

- Ignorance is not evidence.
- Argument is not evidence.
- Unless you have evidence you are merely making a claim.

SUMMARY OF CHAPTER 3

Belief and doubt are bedfellows. They go together. This is very unlike the *doubtless* attitude that we *all* display towards evidential information. Nobody, neither Christian nor 'atheist', doubts that they will fall if they jump out of a second floor window. The absence of doubt in cases like that indicates that those pieces of information (knowns) have transcended the need for belief. They have become accepted as items of unfalsified evidential information; they are, to use Andy's own phrase, 'Things That Are', which no longer need re-affirmation, or active believing.

Doubt goes with belief because we *all* understand that:
- We doubt the beliefs of others, we can, and do, consider their beliefs to be doubtful – merely hypotheses
- Belief is best applied to untested assumptions (that's *why* we can challenge the beliefs of others)
- Active believing is *not* necessary for unfalsified evidential information, for THINGS THAT ARE, for 'knowns'.
- Conversely, the very application of belief to a proposition should reveal the inherently dubious nature of that proposition – the sight of others believing in obvious mumbo jumbo ought to make a belief *less* credible. Yet some pastors have voluntarily died of treatable snake-bite in the expectation that their god will save them!

In the previous chapters we have shown that 'god' is no more than a hypothesis that you can choose to believe in or not. It follows that all the properties and characteristics assigned to 'gods' are also hypothetical; *they are hypotheses about a hypothesis!* (More about this in Chapter 8) It's even worse than that if 'god' is, as claimed, 'immaterial' because 'immateriality' cannot be investigated, so that makes Her an unfalsifiable hypothesis, an *unscientific* hypothesis. A hypothesis is an assumption that hasn't passed testing; an unscientific hypothesis is an *untestable* assumption.

Sadly, the word 'belief' is not serving us very well in the twenty-first century. Do we believe a 'wet paint' sign or do we touch to check? I bet you've been let down by some experience where a belief of yours has turned out to have been mistaken. "I believe I can get the car into that parking space," "I believe this coffee is cool enough to drink," - that sort of thing.

Don't we all doubt the beliefs of others? If we didn't doubt their beliefs we'd go to *their* church/synagogue/mosque/temple, wouldn't we? So we all know that beliefs can be false don't we? In fact, doubt is the wedded partner of belief, isn't it?

Once we realize this simple fact, we can start to regard the act of believing in a more realistic way - as indicative of dubious propositions. This fits with other characteristics that we know about religious beliefs, such as they need active re-affirming, constant reiteration. This is most evident in the ritual behavior required by all faiths: daily prayer, regular ceremonial meetings, dietary taboos or periods of fasting, etc.

I'm not trying to redefine 'belief'; I'm merely drawing attention to how we *already* use it. *"I believe in Gravity"* would be a ridiculous thing to say; that's why nobody says it, anymore than they say, *"I believe in Richard Dawkin's left foot",* to use Andy's example. Conversely, as soon as someone says they believe something, our instinct is to doubt or to disbelieve them. We even disbelieve experts and vote against their advice in elections and referenda if it suits our political persuasion. Belief is, at best, a personally chosen attitude towards a dubious proposition, towards a concept or claim. While at worst it's an inherited position when the choice of belief has been abdicated, in childhood, to parents. It's of trivial importance, this belief stuff, isn't it? A belief is just a chosen opinion about the unknown. Should we be dying for it? Even more pertinently, should we be killing for it? Should we be infecting children with it?

"People are brilliant at creating a narrative from minimal evidence; the brain is a machine for jumping to conclusions".
Philosopher Daniel KAHNEMAN

IN A NUTSHELL

- Propositions are statements expressing something that can be true *or false*.
- 'Concrete facts', which have not been falsified, are *not* candidates for belief. They are 'knowns' and therefore *do not require belief to be assigned to them.*
- Belief is a personal attitude that you can choose to assign to propositions that lack evidence.
- Conversely, any statement that DOES require belief is not a 'concrete fact' but a dubious proposition or hypothesis.
- We need to realize that belief is unimportant.

When we sort propositions into believable or unbelievable we are using the wrong filter: we should be sorting them into evidential (and therefore not requiring belief) or non-evidential (and therefore appropriate for choosing whether to believe or disbelieve them). Belief and disbelief are subsets of non-evidential propositions. *A belief is just a chosen opinion about the unknown.*

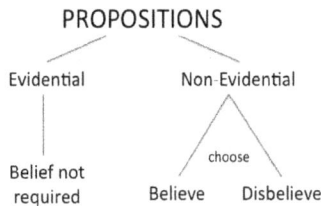

PROPOSITIONS

Evidential   Non-Evidential

|

Belief not   choose

required   Believe   Disbelieve

Opinions are like assholes, everybody's got one.
Clint EASTWOOD

97

Top Ten Signs You Might Be A Fundamentalist Christian

10. You vigorously deny the existence of thousands of gods claimed by other religions, but feel outraged when someone denies the existence of yours.

9. You feel insulted and dehumanized when scientists say that people evolved from other life forms, but you have no problem with the Biblical claim that we were created from dirt.

8. You laugh at polytheists, but you have no problem believing in a Triune God.

7. Your face turns purple when you hear of the atrocities attributed to Allah, but you don't even flinch when hearing about how God/Jehovah slaughtered all the babies of Egypt in Exodus and ordered the elimination of entire ethnic groups in Joshua including women, children, animals and trees!

6. You laugh at Hindu beliefs that deify humans, and Greek claims about gods sleeping with women, but you have no problem believing that the Holy Spirit impregnated Mary, who then gave birth to a man-god who got killed, came back to life and then ascended into the sky.

5. You are willing to spend your life looking for little loopholes in the scientifically established age of Earth (4.6 billion years), but you find nothing wrong with believing dates recorded by Bronze Age tribesmen sitting in their tents and guessing that Earth is only a few generations old.

4. You believe that the entire population of this planet, with

the exception of those who share your beliefs — though excluding those in all rival sects – will spend Eternity in an infinite Hell of Suffering. This fate will even happen to your children if they don't submit to your faith, and yet you consider your religion to be the most tolerant and loving.

3. While modern science, history, geology, biology, and physics have failed to convince you otherwise, some idiot rolling around on the floor speaking in "tongues" may be all the evidence you need to "prove" Christianity.

2. You define 0.01% as a "high success rate" when it comes to answered prayers. You consider that to be sufficient evidence that prayer works. And you think that the remaining 99.99% failure rate was simply the will of God.

1. You actually know a lot less than many atheists and agnostics do about the Bible, Christianity, and church history – but still call yourself a Christian.

(AUTHOR UNKNOWN)

I wouldn't kill myself for my beliefs, I might be wrong.
Bertrand RUSSELL

God made me an atheist.
Who are you to question his wisdom?
Imtiaz MAHMOOD

PART TWO

THE CONSTRUCTION OF A RATIONAL WORLDVIEW

4. **EVIDENCE** *What is it?*

Nothing contributes to epistemology (the study of how we know things) more than evidence. Evidence is behind all of mankind's achievements, such as the International Space Station and my artificial heart valve. We know that Andy Bannister *values* evidence – in The Atheist Who Didn't Exist, he writes:

"So what about God's existence? Well, <u>I'd want</u> to suggest that there is a <u>wealth of evidence</u> that you can engage with to explore that question, ranging from philosophical and scientific <u>arguments</u>, to moral and ethical <u>arguments</u>, to <u>arguments</u> from literature and history, as well as those from <u>personal experience</u>." (My underlinings)

I say, *"Want on, Andy"* because none of the items he lists as a 'wealth of evidence' constitute *actual* evidence at all. He even describes them as *arguments* rather than evidence. Isn't that a clue? Let's face it; you can pay an advocate to argue any proposition... Although he values evidence, Andy doesn't know what it is! I meet this a lot; many theists don't seem to know what evidence actually is and, consequently, they often imagine that they have some when they don't. Christians have offered me parables and poems as evidence! Here's the thing: **arguments**, *whether philosophical, scientific, moral, ethical, or from literature and history are* **not** *evidence;* **neither** *is personal experience.*

101

Evidence must come from *external reality*, not *from the mind* or from any recordings of thoughts and, to be effective, evidence must be *beyond reasonable doubt*. It should be like playing an ace, a killer blow, a cold hard fact. Anything less than that would not be foundational; it would require personal belief; it would be just an individually chosen attitude towards a proposition; it would be merely an opinion and would be doubted, questioned and disagreed with and hence would be worthless. There is little point presenting an item of 'supporting' information and having it disputed; that would achieve nothing. Once an item of information has passed through a brain, there is reason to suspect that it might have been invented, interpreted, edited, misremembered, exaggerated or embellished to suit the brain owner's personal opinion or agenda. Therefore, *all accounts are tainted…*

So what *might* deliver the required standard for evidence?

Let's start by taking a look at *ARGUMENTS*. Firstly, an indictment: *arguments can be wrong*. Andy *knows* this. He even subtitled his book *'The Dreadful Consequences of Bad Arguments'*. There might also be a clue to the fallibility of arguments in some of the synonyms for the word 'argument' – dispute, disagreement, and *quarrel!* We can all have *opinions* about arguments, that's why if you have two philosophers you will probably hear two different philosophies! Would you

102

accept being convicted on dubious grounds of opinion rather than on independently verifiable objective evidence?

Secondly, arguments are purely cerebral – they are conceived inside craniums, they are *thoughts*. Other people can think up ways to refute your thoughts: counter-arguments. Ask yourself, is it likely that thoughts are automatically correct? Even if an argument is logical, the connections have only been made in a brain. For some reason, some people don't realize that what goes on *inside* our heads has no compulsory correspondence to what goes on *outside*. This blind spot is amazing considering all the *obviously* fanciful ideas that human brains have come up with, e.g. Unicorns, Dragons, Pegasus, Humpty Dumpty, Daleks, Penrose's Fork and M C Escher's impossible drawings.

That is why philosophy, great though it is, has its limits. Philosophy is thought up correlations and, as we know from statistics, you can't conclude anything from a correlation other than *'there is a correlation'* – the most famous example links the decline of piracy with the increase in global temperatures!

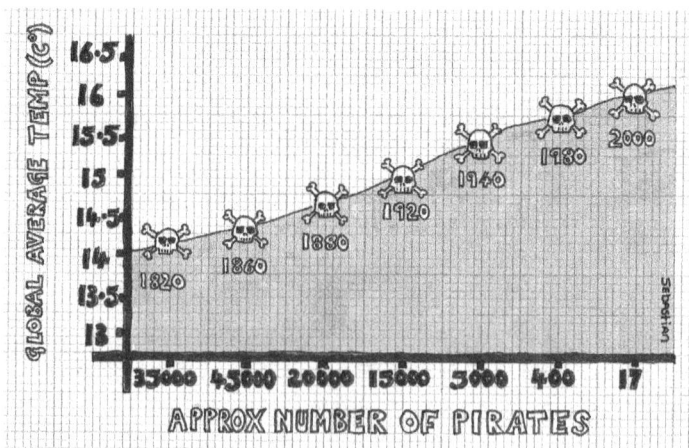

So, how can we tell what *is* correct? We must test thoughts to discover whether they match observations of nature or not. Philosophy is fine when we have nothing else as a source of information, but it is *only* thinking and must *not* be considered to have supremacy over observations of natural reality. It was only when mankind started looking *outwards* for information that progress began to be made. Philosophy is like a glass of urine – if there's no other water it's ok to drink it, but who wouldn't prefer an external source? Surprisingly, many theists are stuck in pre-Renaissance internal-thinking-only mode where checking against observations is not invoked.

The Heavens don't fit   Good old Copernicus! His
Ptolemy's spheres...   Heliocentric model is right!

I have written earlier about the boundless capacity of our brains to conceive ideas both real and fictitious. Being merely thoughts makes arguments *concepts*, not observed facts. Being merely concepts means we can all have *opinions* about them, and we *do*: I know theists who accept *some* of the arguments for 'god' but not *other* arguments for 'god'. For example, the 'ontological argument[44]' doesn't attract support from all believers. One apologist I know said, "I don't think it's a very strong argument." Well, if he can *opine* that one of the arguments for 'god' is not very strong, why can't he recognize the same weakness in all the other arguments – that they are just opinions? The point is simple: arguments are conceptual, they cannot be right or wrong, they can only be weak or strong, they are not evidence, *and evidence is what is needed!* Evidence must be beyond doubt, which puts it *beyond dispute*, but arguments are mired in disagreement. A proposition that can be subjected to differences of opinion is unreliable and is, therefore, not useful as evidence. It's only when an argument is substantiated by repeatable observations that it begins to have value.

Unfortunately, even evidence doesn't give *certainty* because there is always the possibility that *new* evidence may be discovered that doesn't fit the existing model and requires it to be rethought. So *there is no certainty*, only probability, and everything we think we know must be notionally up for permanent review in case new evidence arrives that doesn't correspond with our current model. Our brains crave certainty but asserters of certain knowledge are merely opinionated. Beware of them; they might be dangerous.

Collections of evidential information, which have not been falsified, have enabled the construction of elaborate models of reality (Theories[45]) that match it closely. So, in practice we take those as 'true' - they are as near to the concept of 'true' as we have currently got and, having become evidential, they are *real* as well as conceptual. We live our lives in the supposition that they are facts, to the extent of not needing to actively believe in them.

I wish I knew what *grounds* theists use for making their selections of which unevidenced argument to *believe* and which unevidenced argument to *disbelieve*; can it be just *personal choice?* What's the value of that? I choose coffee with cream but without sugar, but I don't make it into my 'belief system' or worldview! It pays to remember that, in a universe where nothing is absolutely certain, what matters is not 'truth' but whether information has been falsified or not (see philosopher Karl Popper[46]). If it hasn't been falsified, then it may be considered to have currently transcended the need for active belief: it has become a 'known'. That's as close as we can get to 'true'.

It's worse than a mere lack of observations, because several Creator Deity concepts simply cannot *be* investigated. For example, we don't have any means of detecting the immaterial, and if we ever do detect something immaterial, it would immediately have to be reclassified as material!

Is there any evidence for eternity? If eternity is permissible, couldn't the universe be eternal in some sense too? Theists love the badly named 'Big Bang'[47] since it seems to confirm their assertion that the universe had an origin, but there remains the possibility that the universe bounces eternally from origin to extinction and on to the next origin, etc. Perhaps we are just in the latest iteration. The truth is no-one knows, but theists are afraid of admitting that. It would mean abandoning their beliefs as unimportant: a big price to pay.

That discussion is beyond the scope of this book but in particular, there is no evidence for *past* eternity. Even top Christian apologist, William Lane Craig, accepts that there is no past eternity but he doesn't apply this belief to 'god'. Instead, he claims that 'god' is somewhere other than in material reality or that reality includes a portion that is unreal! Either way is an Ad Hoc Fallacy. Look here for a mathematical proof (i.e. a conceptualization) that indicates there is no such thing as past eternity: http://tinyurl.com/cwbtaq3

The theists' response to this type of questioning is to assert that the creator must be *'outside'* the universe where it *is* possible to be eternal! Of course that's just a claim. Nowadays we should recognize that all arguments are merely concepts fabricated in the brain and that they need testing to discover whether they accurately model the universe or not. In other words, we need evidence, not just arguments. Testing trumps thinking. So, investigations must be conducted to see if observations match the claim of a 'creator deity' and, so far, no evidence has been observed for any of the following concepts: Eternity, Absoluteness, Infinity, Immateriality, A Supernatural Realm, A Creator Deity, Tinker Bell...

If, as many Christians assert, a complex universe needs an intelligent designer, why does the designer itself not need an even more intelligent designer? You might reasonably think that the argument that complexity indicates design must apply to the intelligent designer Herself. Since a designer is necessarily more complex than what it designs, surely She needs a designer *more* than the cosmos does. This leads to an infinite regression of *increasing complexity* – like a Russian doll with ever larger dolls inside!

That's the complete opposite to what we actually find! Looking backwards through time, the universe gets more and more *simple* until, at the supposed beginning, no matter exists; *not even matter!* These are exactly the wrong conditions under which to expect to discover a being more complex than the entire present day, utterly vast, universe that has taken almost 13.8 billion years to develop! In the absence of matter, what would its complexity be made of? Ask yourself, are they just shoehorning-in a favorite presupposition? Isn't that an example of the Begging the Question Fallacy?

And postulating that the designer is eternal and therefore didn't need to be designed, is just Special Pleading or an Ad Hoc Fallacy – it's a Get Out of Jail Free card. Please also note that the universe having an origin would *not* be evidence for a creation event *by a supernatural creator deity of any kind*, let alone a specifically *Christian* one. The discovery of a beginning tells us nothing about *how* it was started; all we can do is guess (hypothesize) about that.

Here's an example of a *real* origin: the island of Surtsey[48] appeared off the coast of Iceland in 1967; it had an entirely natural beginning. It was due to an undersea volcanic eruption, not to creation by a supernatural deity. In fact, every question we have succeeded in answering has turned out to have an entirely natural explanation like that. That makes 'godunnit' a *highly improbable unscientific hypothesis.*

The reality is there is a lack of evidence on the subject of how the universe came about and, without evidence, all we can do is hypothesize. Theists hypothesize on the basis of their presupposition of 'god', while scientists do it on the basis of what is actually *known*, what is evidential. Arguments are useful for backing a hypothesis or for designing an investigation but they can do nothing to convert a hypothesis into a conclusion – that takes evidence.

Where some keen apologist philosophers go wrong is in assuming that an outcome of logical reasoning is the end of the story. It's not. It's only the end of *conceptualizing*. They have only produced a mental construct. In scientific terms that is known as a hypothesis or informed guess. Without any supporting evidence from reality, it is merely an idea. In fact, the very *same* logic can often be used to make a case for a counter argument, as you will see in Stephen Law's Evil God Challenge. All the same arguments can be used for the existence of an evil 'god' as for a good 'god'. So, if you're going to claim that your arguments 'are evidence', you must accept that 'god' is not necessarily good! Do you want that? See http://tinyurl.com/ht9wgrl

Conceptualization is just the *beginning* of the *next* stage - testing to see if your hypothesis matches observations. Scientific investigation is like saying to the universe, "I have this idea, it sounds logical to me, is it correct?" We then need to conduct an investigation and, if observations support the outcome of the syllogism, they turn it into a conclusion. If they don't, it remains merely a hypothesis. This revelation about the lower value of *thought alone* as compared to *thought tested by observation* occurred during the Renaissance and unleashed a massive acceleration in the rate of discovery of information. It's why I can write this book on my laptop.

Without investigating for a match with reality, philosophy remains just thought. It's internally produced. It's rather like urine... In desperation it's perfectly safe to drink urine but we all know that an external source of water is preferable!

Even a scientific conclusion is only a *provisional* end. There is always the possibility that new evidence may arrive in the future that won't fit the original conclusion. This is why scientists do not claim *certainty*. It's only theists (and bad journalists) who claim to have unalterable, certain knowledge and they do so *without any evidence!* We have never discovered anything that is definitely absolute in reality. Even Absolute Zero has never been observed and it's mathematically possible to have negative temperatures! Furthermore any proposition that *cannot* be tested is an *unscientific hypothesis* doomed to remain merely hypothetical until some new means of investigation becomes available. An 'immaterial god' comes into this category.

Arguments require supporters and we are all entitled to decide whether to support an argument or not, but popular agreement does not equal veracity, that would be the Vox Populis Fallacy. Taking polls does not discover truth. Although it may give backing to a hypothesis, an argument cannot confer certainty of the truth of a proposition about reality. Until they have been tested against observations, arguments are just matters of opinion, thoughts are just thoughts. This is why philosophers are famous for disagreeing! Arguments are definitely *not* conclusions; they are not *even* evidence.

As we have seen, a correlation is not merely *no indication of causation* but it cannot be relied upon to have any additional information beyond the correlating factor. We need to understand the *mechanism* of connection between a cause and an effect before we can accept causality. So why can't theists understand that conceptualizations, where a correlation has only been conceived in a brain, have no automatic right to explain aspects of nature?

It's important to realize that arguments are only ideas. Think of it like this: the word 'tree' is used to represent a large woody plant but it isn't identical with a tree (it depends on the language being used for a start). It is symbolic of a tree, a representation of it. Similarly, a two dimensional drawing can look like a three dimensional subject, but it isn't a clone of it, it's a representation of it. Another example: a mathematical formula can describe the symmetry of a starfish, but it isn't a starfish, it's a representation of a starfish shape. The same is true of arguments, they are mental concepts that attempt to represent reality but they are *not* reality and the representation *may or may not* be accurate. We must not mistake *representations of reality* for reality itself, that's like mistaking the map for the territory.

Another clue comes from the fact that the effectiveness of an argument depends on how clever you are at *expressing* it, (that's why we pay good advocates a lot of money) while evidence in the form of repeatable observation is not affected by how clever a communicator you are: everyone can see it for themselves.

Ok, some arguments include some premises that are real scientific conclusions, being supported by evidence, but there is always a question mark over the *outcome* of the syllogism, which has only been connected *inside* a brain or brains. It needs investigating for correspondence with reality in the form of observations from the universe. Every step of a syllogism needs backing up with observation. Whether abduction, deduction or induction has been involved we only have a mental construct until testing against nature has been achieved by the gathering of observed evidence. (Never forget that the evidence is only as good as the *most recently observed data* on the situation.)

So, the *only* way to discover information, such as whether there is a creator (presumably believers would like their deity to be *real?*) is this process of investigating for evidence. Evidence comes in the form of repeatable observations. Logic can help with the formulation of hypotheses and with deciding how to investigate, but it cannot confirm anything without evidence. The gulf is between the 'Conceptual Realm' *inside* the head, and the Natural Realm *outside* of it.

True, it would be great if we could just sit down and make up arguments that would automatically be correct, but verification only happens when a hypothesis is confirmed by observations. Every person who uses logic should know that

115

logic cannot confirm anything to be true. It can only falsify a proposition. If ever you find yourself thinking that a logical outcome must be correct, go and investigate the double slit experiment: https://www.youtube.com/watch?v=DfPeprQ7oGc

Scientists *do* employ arguments – they're particularly useful for supporting hypotheses. A famous example is the argument for the existence of extraterrestrial intelligent life forms. This is based on the Drake Equation, which has two premises:

1. There are an estimated two hundred billion galaxies[49], each with about two hundred billion stars (suns[50]) many of them with planets, as we are just discovering (probably 10 to the power of 22 in number, see here http://exoplanets.org); some of these planets are in the 'Goldilocks Zone'[51] where water exists as liquid, which is conducive to the existence of life.
2. 13.8 billion years[47] have passed since the Big Bang.[47]

With so many potentially habitable locations and so much past time, it is highly probable that intelligent beings (like us[52]?) have evolved many times over and in many places. Well, that's fine and logical, as far as it goes, but nobody takes that as *evidence* for the existence of alien intelligence. It's just a claim, an opinion, an argument, a hypothesis, *a belief,* and therefore should be 'tested to destruction'. For one thing, how can anyone be sure that life can start easily, even if all the ingredients and conditions needed are present?

However, based on The Drake Equation, the Search for Extra-Terrestrial Intelligence (SETI) was instigated back in the 1960s. No evidence has been discovered so far, which means that the hypothesis, based on the argument, remains unconfirmed. It hasn't become a conclusion yet. So intelligent aliens are in the same dubious state as 'gods' – they are all currently hypotheses awaiting evidence. But at least we can be 100% sure life *can* exist in the universe because *we* are an example of it. Ask yourself; can the same be said of any gods? Drake's argument, in the form of a statistical calculation, is not taken as evidence. We are *searching* for evidence. Evidence would come in the form of *observations*.

Here are some more examples: on Thursday, 11th February 2016, a hypothesis suddenly became a conclusion: Gravitational waves[53] were observed. No magic was involved in this transformation from concept to fact, just two scientific instruments – LIGOs (acronym: Laser Interferometer Gravitational-Wave Observatory). The previous time this happened was on 4th July 2012 when the ATLAS detector (acronym: A Toroidal LHC ApparatuS) at the Large Hadron Collider at CERN (the European organization for Nuclear Research) picked up observations of the formerly hypothetical Higgs Boson[54]. Again it was observations, not logic that wrought the change from an untested hypothesis to a conclusion. That's how mere hypotheses become evidential information - by *observing*, not by logic, nor by miracles.

In both cases arguments had been made for their existence, but that did *not* mean that gravitational waves or the Higgs Boson had become accepted as real; arguments are not evidence. To highlight a contrast, not only has no credible observation for an immaterial 'god' ever been made, but also no instrument for the detection of such a 'god' has even been designed, let alone constructed. We have no idea how to detect the 'immaterial' so there is little chance of confirming or denying its existence. Ask yourself, is the claim that 'god' is 'immaterial' just an ad hoc fallacy intended to 'support' a hypothetical deity that lacks evidence?

The process of discovery usually goes like this:
Question > Hypothesis > Observations > Conclusion.

Whereas theistic thinking seems to be:
Presupposition > Argument > Conclusion.

That's just *wrong*. We have known that is wrong since The Renaissance.
(I'm using 'conclusion' in the sense of an outcome verified by evidence in the form of shareable repeatable observations.)

118

So, here is the current situation:

- The origin of the universe is unexplained; it's an area of ignorance that is under investigation. It's a *question*. Questions are not answers. Ignorance is not an answer: you cannot 'deduce' that 'we dunno' means 'godunnit'.
- So 'god' remains merely a **hypothesis**.
- An 'immaterial' god cannot be investigated so 'god' is an **unscientific hypothesis**.
- Every question we have succeeded in answering so far has turned out to have a natural explanation, not a supernatural one; therefore 'god' is a **highly improbable cause or explanation**.

Religious beliefs often have to be protected by outlawing disagreement and threatening to punish dissenters. Their perpetrators need to do this because arguments are not conclusive. They are not conclusive because they are just conceptual: they have not been supported by evidence yet. Once they have acquired evidence, there will be *no* argument. Protecting an argument by attempting to silence disagreement is a sure sign of the dubiousness of a proposition. Religions protect themselves in this way with laws for the bogus crimes of blasphemy, heresy and apostasy. Sometimes the punishment for violation is death. The need for protection by threats of dismissal or death should be a clue as to the dubious nature of belief claims.

119

A VICAR WAS FIRED FOR HERESY IN SUSSEX IN 1994

Vicar Anthony Freeman said, *"God is not a supernatural being but merely the sum of all our values and ideals"* and was dismissed from his parish for heresy by the Bishop of Chichester.

~~~

Now let's take a look at *PERSONAL EXPERIENCE*. I'm going to tell you a personal story... *Before he died, in 1973, I remember my grandfather telling me how he once drove Queen Victoria in one of the first 'horseless carriages' on the Isle of Wight.* Do you choose to believe that?

If not, why not? My story contains several references that are plausible – we know the Isle of Wight exists (I was born there) and that Queen Victoria had Osborne House[55] built as her holiday home. We also know that early cars existed before her death in 1901 and that my grandfather was a young man at the time (that much is evidential – there are birth records). So have I just made up my experience of him telling me about that incident? How would you know?

To be honest, I can't actually be sure of the details myself. It was a very long time ago, I was quite young and I may have forgotten the details. Did Gramp say he drove the Queen herself or one of her entourage? The Queen certainly spent her summers at Osborne House, which is near to where Gramp lived... Naturally, I *want* to believe that Gramp was telling me the truth, but he was very old when he told me and Queen Victoria died when he was very young; he could have misremembered the event himself. Was it really *him* driving the veteran vehicle or was it someone he knew? Was he glorifying the event in an attempt to impress? Ask yourself, how would we know? Is there a license to exaggerate in the interests of giving a good story-telling performance? It's certainly permissible for comedians to stretch the truth in the cause of getting a laugh; everyone wants to be well received.

Does the genuine continued existence of Osborne House confirm events that are alleged to have happened there? I think not: locations are one thing – there are traces of

Nazareth, but *specific historical events* cannot be verified in detail without a time machine. Ask yourself, what sort of archeological discovery could confirm a 'virgin birth'? The movie 'Muppets Most Wanted' features scenes filmed in Dublin and the Tower of London, does that make it *true*? Some theists have a tendency to leap from actual physical remains to faith in miracles! That's like saying Lapland really exists so there must be a Santa Claus!

Let's face it people can claim to have experienced all sorts of unlikely happenings. Camille James Harman believes she has experience of being abducted by aliens many times. President George W. Bush tells us he experienced 'god' telling him to invade Iraq and Afghanistan[56]. Joseph Smith claimed to have experienced a vision of the Angel Moroni[57] directing him where to dig to find the golden plates bearing the text of the Book of Mormon. William Blake[58] asserted that he saw angels in a tree near his home in Felpham, West Sussex, where he lived when writing his inspirational poem 'Jerusalem', which was later turned into an anthem with Charles Parry's majestically stirring musical setting. *We can all form our own opinions about the experiences they described.* Ask yourself, should we consider them to be evidence? I doubt it. Like William Blake, I also get 'visions'. I know that it's just the migraine aura but it makes me realize that my senses and brain, my *own* experiences, are untrustworthy. I can't believe *myself,* let alone *you!*

You see the difficulty with experiences? They don't travel. Personal experiences, such as 'revelations', are just that - *personal* – they cannot be shared. Can you share my grief? Or my pain? What about my orgasm? Experiences may seem real, but they only seem real to *one person*. They rely on perception, interpretation, judgment and memory, so they are subjective. The trouble with the subjective is the only transmission method is by means of words so we are immediately into reportage, which can be influenced by the reporter's agenda.

We all recognize that *other* people can be unreliable witnesses so we take their reports with pinches of salt. Even police identification parades are now accepted to be of limited value because it has been discovered that 1 in 50 of us is face blind[59]. Our courts acknowledge this and do not put much credence in uncorroborated witness accounts because we know they are very subjective. Sadly, courts make major mistakes so they are a bad example of how to discover 'truth'. Recent research reveals how easy it is to plant false memories in a person's mind[60]. We are really very inaccurate and unreliable witnesses and our testimony cannot be trusted. Experiences are simply not transferable as evidence.

On the subject of court justice, have you ever asked yourself why courts won't accept supernatural defense claims? You won't escape conviction by asserting, "Wasn't me: godunnit!" It will be assumed that you committed the crime of your own free will. 'God' may be assigned credit for life-saving surgery on the grounds that She gave the surgeons their brains, but a *criminal's* brain is *not* assumed to be 'god' given! Ask yourself, is this selective application of 'god's' involvement intended to suit the assumption of a *good* god? *Surgery is part of god's plan, but theft is due to 'fallen' man's free will! The Christian 'god' can't be involved with the nefarious, can She! She doesn't plan 'sin'!* (I've italicized the irony.) Ask yourself, isn't this Special Pleading for 'god'?

At this point, theists sometimes try to claim that everything is an experience, including a scientist making observations and, therefore, they say, subjective judgment ruins the objectivity of reporting data. If I were writing this in an earlier century I would have had to agree with them. Back in history the imagination *did* intrude upon observation. Primitive microscopes enabled Nicolaas Hartsoeker to postulate a 'homunculus'[61] in a sperm and an early telescope used by the Italian astronomer Giovanni Schiaparelli in 1877 enabled him to picture 'canals' on Mars[62].

Today, things are different: we use *multiple independent repeated observations* to eliminate subjectivity *and* human sense organs are rarely involved. We now have autonomous robots that can make observations on distant planets or their moons (and even on a comet). Instruments can collect data that is outside the range detectable by human senses and can produce a digital electronic output that can be evaluated statistically by a computer with little human involvement. As artificial intelligence gradually enables computers to respond to sensory input and for example, drive cars, we have to wonder will men soon be completely out of the loop of discovery?

The objectivity of observations these days is even true at the quantum level as the following paragraph by Lawrence Krauss[63], writing in the New York Times shows:

125

Entanglement is so spooky that it's tempting, when thinking about it, to draw nonsensical conclusions. Deepak Chopra, for example, keeps implying that quantum mechanics means that objective reality doesn't exist apart from conscious experience. The truth, however, is that consciousness is irrelevant to the act of measurement, which can be done by machines, or even by single photons. If consciousness matters, then the inner thoughts of the experimenter who operates the machines would also have to be reported when we write up the results of our experiments. We'd need to know whether they were daydreaming about sex, for example. We don't. The machines can record data and print it out whether or not a person is in the room, and those printouts, which behave classically, don't change when the humans come back.

~~~

So, returning to the opening paragraph of this chapter, if what Andy *imagines* is evidence, his sources of 'verification', to whit, arguments and experience, are not *actually* evidence at all, then, *what is?*

Well, it's simply **information that people cannot reasonably express a contrary opinion about.** It's indisputable facts and propositions that *do not require evaluating for belief.* That's why scientists insist on repeating observations and experiments. It's not just the *discoverer's* eyes that we have to believe then, *it's lots of people's eyes* including, if at all possible, *our own!* Repeatability eliminates opinion; the data becomes as close to objective as possible – it becomes *evidence*. You can't argue with it.

Let's imagine your father brought you up to believe in Zeus[64]. When you were a small child you simply believed what you were told by your trusted Dad, but in teenage you started to question things, to seek actual evidence. You realized that it's possible to have different opinions about all that knowledge you had been given about Zeus. His statue could be just a sculptor's vision, his drawings just an artist's impression, his scriptures just writer's tales, and then you might have formed the opinion that there was no evidence for Zeus. *Did* you come to that conclusion? Are you an 'atheist' towards Zeus? *You poor, immoral, purposeless, Zeus-hating heathen, you!*

In the absence of evidence, different people form different opinions, different beliefs. Therefore, the existence of widely differing opinions (beliefs) reveals a dearth of evidence. This lack of evidence is why, for example, there can be several different explanations for how the Big Bang might have come about: String theory[65] (actually it's a hypothesis), Multiverse[66], Creation (yes, I'm including it in the list!), Big Bounce, etc. This lack of evidence also explains why there are so many different 'gods', different religions and different sects. There are about 38,000 different Christian denominations alone! Ask yourself, why is that? Well, now you know; it's due to the lack of evidence for *any* 'god'. Of course, if any 'god' *did have* evidence, argument would cease and all the other 'gods' would be discredited. But that's not the case: Yahweh, Allah, Jesus, Shiva, Buddha, and more, all still have their believers.

For comparison, let's take a look at something that *has* gained credibility and ask ourselves what it is about it that has given it veracity. Gravity is a good example: anyone, anywhere, at any time can repeatedly observe its effects. We can measure it with instruments – the force is slightly less on top of large mountains and at the equator compared to the poles: you are further from the Earth's core in those locations (the Earth is wider than it is tall, tomato-shaped not lemon-shaped). The existence of the force of gravity is robustly re-observable and not dependent on the testimony of the personal experiences of others, or on arguments and opinions. It's objective and not contentious. *That's evidence.*

Evidence must have the following properties: **it must be observable, repeatedly,** by anyone (with access to appropriate equipment), anywhere and at any time (within reason), and **it must be external** (not just a concept in a head), which means **it must be shareable** – *you* need to be able to observe it for yourself so you don't have to believe anyone's report. Anything offered as 'evidence', that has its source in a person, such as reports (written or spoken), appeals to authority, testimony or witnessing, is *not* acceptable as evidence. Once a person is involved in the transmission of information it becomes vulnerable to his agenda, it becomes blended with his opinion. This is why the Royal Society[67] chose as its motto 'Nullius in verba' ('nothing in words' or 'take nobody's word for it'). Scientific reports are very boring to read because they have to be written as objectively as possible; there are rules to follow to keep them unbiased and dispassionate.

Ask yourself; does anyone have a different opinion about the effect of gravity here on Earth? No! There is agreement on only *one* model of gravity – the model that tells us to beware of the possibility of falling. That's why evidential information does not require belief; we all accept that it just *is*. It belongs to the 'THINGS THAT ARE' category, as Andy described them. The reliance on evidence in the form of repeatable observations is what makes scientific method such a powerful and effective tool. It's why I can use this laptop...

Evidence supports single undisputed explanations of aspects of reality. These are very unlike the multitude of conflicting faith-based explanations for phenomena. Ask yourself; does the huge number of those different faiths possibly indicate that they are just matters of opinion? What do you think? Ask yourself, can't we often tell the difference between probable truths on the one hand and claims (beliefs) on the other, simply because the known is the only option on the menu?

You might protest that scientific investigation is not the only way of knowing things. I would ask you to provide examples of other ways of knowing (crystal ball gazing not accepted). You might say that science can't explain everything. I agree, but I would add the word 'yet', and I would caution that there may be some things that are unknowable. Science is a work in progress. Who knows what we might discover in the future? Only a fool would claim that science has the answer to everything right *now*, but think about it, all of the achievements and advances made by mankind are thanks to the scientific style of working even if, at the time of discovery, they didn't know that the procedure they were using was going to become called 'scientific method'.

Also, it's fine to say 'I don't know' in science because scientists try to be scrupulously honest about such things. It's okay for a scientist to say he doesn't know what caused the Big Bang. It's preferable to making some unsupportable claim which risks being revealed as just a bluff.

Whereas, asserting 'godunnit' isn't in any sense an explanation at all. It's just trying to turn a lack of knowledge into an answer. Worse than that, it's claiming to have knowledge that you don't really have. We call that a deception. Any scientist attempting that tactic would soon be professionally discredited (see Fleischmann and Pons[68]), and accepting donations when making unfounded claims should be the criminal offence of obtaining money on false pretences. Selling snake oil. Fraud. For purely historical reasons, religions get a free pass from that law.

You can have lower standards of what you count as 'evidence' if you wish, but then you might risk being deceived (wanna buy London Bridge?) and you will certainly be in disagreement with those who have different opinions about the validity of your sources. You won't have those problems if you adopt the high standard of evidence that I described above, based on shareable repeatable observations.

You might say, as others have done, that scientific standards of evidence only apply *within* the field of science. That would expose you as having a basic misconception about science: *you assume that science is a subject with a boundary.* It's not. It's a *method*: a prescription for investigation that can potentially be applied wherever there are questions to be answered. Whereas you *can* say that English is about words, Math is about numbers and History is about the past, you *can't* define Science by what it's *about*. In principle, Science is a *process*, an *activity,* not a field of study. It's 'about' anything

131

and everything to which scientific techniques can be applied, and that list grows as we invent new tools for investigation; the microscope opened up a huge field that became called microscopy.

Here are some of the branches of science: geology, paleontology, archeology, biochemistry, fluidics, aeronautics, neurology, genetics, radio astronomy, microbiology, etc. You *can* say what a *branch* of science is about. Every specialism *applies* scientific methods to specific areas of investigation. Each is about a particular topic with a roughly defined border, but the *general principles* of scientific methods of investigation are applicable to any subject area from archeology to zoology. They can even be useful in criminology, music and the dating of theological documents.

Are there any subject areas that are 'off limits' to the application of scientific methods? No. Are there any restrictions to the potential application of scientific methods? Maybe not. Just give us a little time for the development of the appropriate detector technology. For example, Neurology has burgeoned since the invention of Positron Emission Tomography and functional Nuclear Magnetic Resonance. We are inventing gravity wave 'telescopes' for observing massive events in the universe; another new branch of science. Who knows what we will be able to do in the future?

Andy is a believer in two sorts of stuff – matter and 'something else', which he might call 'immaterial' and I would call unreal. One of his chapters is called:

The Lunatic in the Louvre (or: Why Science Cannot Explain the Entirety of Reality)

Andy's PhD is in Islamic Studies, but he is claiming that he knows more about the 'entirety of reality' than scientists do! Ask yourself, is he outside of his specialism? He reckons he has knowledge of a piece of reality that is unknown to science! How does he distinguish this 'immaterial' realm from Fairyland? And do you spot the implied ad hominem of scientists' stupidity in his use of the word 'lunatic'?

Andy digs himself in by writing another parable, this time about a fictitious man named 'Claude' on a visit to the Louvre. Andy makes 'Claude' look silly by having him attempt to answer questions about Leonardo's motivation for painting the Mona Lisa by examining the wood it's painted on! Who would do that? You might be able to determine something about the *age* of an artwork from that, by matching the tree rings with the database, but you can deduce nothing about an *artist's motivation*. He writes that story to make scientists look stupid. It's malicious; it's yet another attempt to ridicule 'atheists'. He implies that 'Claude' is foolishly thinking that science can answer *any* question. Andy claims that 'Claude' is inspired to

133

think in this 'scientistic' way because of a statement by Nobel prize winning chemist Harry Kroto who he quotes as saying:

"Science is the only philosophical construct we have to determine truth with any degree of reliability"

It's rather sad that it suits Andy's agenda to misrepresent Kroto's statement to be a claim that science can answer *all* questions. No sane scientist would claim that. Ask yourself, is that what the quote means? I can read and it doesn't mean that to me! It actually says that science is the *only reliable way* we have of *finding out*. *'Only philosophical construct we have to determine the truth with any reliability'* does not mean that *all* questions are answerable. There may be some *unanswerable* questions. Ask yourself, how would we know? *How can we ever know the discoverability of what we don't know?*

Yes, scientists *do* have a problem with the 'Supernatural' and the 'Immaterial'. Currently those purely conceptual 'realms' cannot be investigated: we don't have any instruments. It's especially difficult because these 'realms' are *defined* as undetectable! So far, all attempts to hunt such phantoms have failed, but think about it, if we ever *do* invent technology that can detect the 'Immaterial', the moment such a ghost is actually observed it will have materialized – become *real!*

Ask yourself; doesn't that suggest that 'immateriality' is probably just a fanciful notion rather than a part of reality? How would we distinguish it from Fantasyland? Theists are imagining a whole 'realm' of *unreality* that they want to categorize as an invisible part of reality! Andy is claiming that this undetectable, *probably imaginary*, concept is part of *'the Entirety of Reality'!* Ask yourself, who is the unrealistic one? And who would want a *discovered* deity – one that is merely *normal?* A 'god' who is material like themselves? How would priests be able to earn off Him without being able to promise 'godly' concepts like 'heaven' and 'salvation', etc.?

Christians seem to deny the accepted definition of 'immaterial', which is 'not made of matter', and favor their *own* meaning, which seems to be *'something that is part of everything but not part of nature'!* Ask yourself; are those concepts of the 'immaterial' just imaginary refuges in which to hide other non-evidential claims like there is a 'creator deity'?

135

And what exactly *is* a 'god' anyway?

Harking back to the beginning of this section on experience, if my unreliable recollection of my grandfather's tale is not a credible source, how much *less* credible are the scriptural accounts of ancient events? Especially considering that it is *accepted even by Christian theologians* that we have no evidence of the gospel stories being written down until decades after the events they report allegedly took place. They also acknowledge that the writers were not present at the events themselves or were not even born at the time! So, someone told somebody then somebody told someone else and so on until the story eventually reached the first scribes. That's hearsay. It would be laughed out of court.

Furthermore, the language changed from Aramaic to Greek along the way! Don't we all know how yarns get 'improved' in the retelling? Why do you think we have expressions like 'fisherman's tale' and 'Chinese whispers'? In fact, we can now trace the likely path that these oral myths took as they spread across the globe, see here http://tinyurl.com/jrgv9d8

Storytellers desire to be popular with their audience so it's hardly surprising that the lead character developed super-powers along the way! All of this is not to mention the fact that, much later, the 'scriptural' texts underwent multiple translations, edits and rewritings in the hundreds of years since *or* the fact that some of the accounts describe events that defy the Laws of Physics! Don't forget, also, *Nullius in verba* – take nobody's word for it... All of this tells us why there is no point arguing about the Bible.

This is why I admire Andy Bannister for *not* constantly quoting the Bible like so many other apologists do. Ancient religious texts have nothing to contribute to the debate on the existence of 'god'. Although I doubt *that* is Andy's reason for refraining from quoting his 'holy' book! However, if we were to regard the Bible as a credible source, why should we not consider the Qur'an, The Torah, the Vedas and The Book of Mormon also to be true? They have their supporters too...

Whether god exists or not is, indeed, a crucial question. Until She can be shown to exist evidentially, any claims about Her nature, abilities, intentions, emotions or attitudes towards us, are a bit premature to say the least. The expression 'Wishful Thinking' springs to mind. Whether you believe the 'god' hypothesis or not will remain a question of individual choice until proper evidence is discovered, and *which* 'god' you choose will be, at best, a personal opinion.

Other people will have different opinions about 'god' and they will form rival religions or sects to yours. Unless you all realize the *unimportance* of your beliefs (claims), disagreement will grow between you until it turns into demonization and, ultimately, into conflict. It is this divisive nature of faiths, founded merely on hypotheses, which makes me conclude that religions are *unnecessary* causes of more harm than good. Watch the news tonight to see if I'm right...

There's another type of pseudo-evidence that theists often claim gives 'support' for their beliefs. It goes like this: we don't know how life began/how the universe originated/where morality comes from, therefore godunnit! Scientists call this 'The God of The Gaps' argument. It's tantamount to saying, "I don't know what next week's winning lottery number will be, but my favorite number is 793,428 so it must be that"! A parallel illustration would be: *the body of an obviously murdered man is discovered, we don't know who the culprit is, therefore godunnit!* Why theists don't use that example...?

138

What's so difficult to understand about 'we don't know'? Do theists think that questions are answers? Do they think that ignorance is evidence? Haven't they noticed that these gaps in our knowledge have been shrinking under the onslaught of scientific investigation? We no longer need to invoke a 'rain god' to explain rain. Ask yourself, isn't that a clue?

So what *would* constitute evidence for 'god'? How about direct observations of 'god' Herself, or even indirect observations – traces left behind by 'god', or genuine miracles, like the re-growth of amputated limbs, especially if they were repeatedly observed and recorded by different instruments or different observers at different locations on different occasions. Most especially if they were benevolent humanitarian rescues from disaster as a direct result of specific prayers, such as the pushing back of lava into a volcano by an invisible hand to save a village, rather than just conjuring tricks like turning water into wine.[69] But we'd still be left with the possibility that some advanced technology was responsible (it's possible that scientists will soon discover how to re-grow limbs by transferring the ability from lizards that possess it), or that we were hallucinating, or witnessing a skilled illusionist in action...

Any sufficiently advanced technology is indistinguishable from magic.
Arthur C. CLARKE

The following is an unknown author's thoughts on what might constitute evidence for 'god'.

All you need to do is give me three things:
1. A coherent definition of God.
2. A set of empirically testable and falsifiable predictions based on the supposition that God exists.
3. Test results that match those predictions and are more parsimoniously explained by God's existence than any other hypothesis.
To date, apologists have failed to meet even the first requirement.

Here on Earth, scientific discovery is proceeding exponentially. If my own father were to be resurrected with all his knowledge of wartime aircraft manufacture, and was shown the satnav on my car windscreen that can vocally direct me to my destination, he might think it was magic. Now that we are developing machine learning and bionic eyes the future seems unlimited. Who knows what scientists will eventually be able to achieve? Artificial Abiogenesis? Bionic Hybrid Humans? Autonomous Humanoid Robots? Terraforming Mars? An Artificial Planet? Everlasting Life? Something we haven't even thought of yet?

Ask yourself; what is there to dislike about non-belief? Do the most secular countries have the highest rate of crime? (They don't[70]). Do you fear non-believing suicide bombers? Haven't you noticed that no 'atheist' kills anyone for being the wrong type of 'atheist'? Are you scared of terrorists inspired by no 'god' and the promise of no virgins in no heavenly afterlife? Really?

Oddly, having touched on what he considers to be *a wealth of evidence'* for 'god' (it isn't), Andy then leaves the subject to a couple of references and speculates about the godly origin of morality and beauty! Why should we read the rest of Andy's book? Surely, his opinions on these matters are just worthless speculation until he has actually established that his Christian deity genuinely exists, aren't they? Currently She's no more real than Star Trek aliens or fairies, which were believed by some to be 'wish granting spirits' as recently as a hundred or so years ago. Ask yourself, what value is a belief?

141

'God' is an unsubstantiated hypothesis. That's the normal condition for hypotheses. It's not 'worse than wrong'; it's simply routine for propositions to be in need of evidence. If its falsifiability can't even be tested, a hypothesis is unscientific. So, 'god' is just such an unscientific hypothesis, and She will remain that way all the while She is proposed to be 'immaterial', unless we can invent a technology to investigate that 'realm', and if we succeed in doing that, She would immediately cease to be immaterial...

The lack of evidence for god leaves believers with no option but to challenge the notion that scientific method is the only means of obtaining information. Do they imagine that disrespecting a reliable source of information somehow adds up to positive evidence for their own unsubstantiated claims?

I sometimes get accused of using philosophy to deny philosophy, of constructing a concept to disprove a concept. That is true, since we can only communicate by means of language, which is entirely conceptual. However, only one side of this argument has a correspondence to reality – the side with the evidence – materialism in this case. You may ask: what is this evidence? It's the enormous pile of explanations for real phenomena that scientific method has gathered over recent centuries and is still discovering today. It's this very laptop that I'm writing on.

Logic is just the 'entry exam' for the process of discovering information. Some applicants will fail. One thought can beat another. After this initial conceptualizing comes the gathering of evidence leading to 'graduation', which requires passing a much tougher test - whether the outcome of conceptualizing matches observations of nature or not. That's how a thought can become a conclusion. It's the only way.

This is my question to all Christian apologists: *Now that you've done your thinking, made your argument for your 'god' and arrived at the outcome of your reasoning, are you going to conduct an investigation to check whether the result of your conceptualizations match reality or not? If not, why not? If your answer is 'no' then you will stay in your thought bubble with your Bible.*

~~~

A philosophical outcome says, 'I have spotted an association between two ideas'
A scientific conclusion says, 'Observations show that nature matches the predicted model'
A belief is just a chosen opinion about the unknown.

SUMMARY OF CHAPTER 4

In chapter 3 on Belief we showed that 'gods' are just hypotheses. *Unscientific* hypotheses if they are, as claimed, 'immaterial'. In this chapter on Evidence we have shown that evidence must be shareable, repeatable, objective observations of nature that are beyond reasonable dispute.

Experiences are *not* evidence because experiences are unshareable subjective events, and arguments are *not* useful as evidence because they are concepts that are open to opinion. Therefore, arguments and experiences do not meet a standard that can be used to support the proposition that a 'god' exists. Until genuine repeatedly observable evidence is discovered, *'god' will remain just a hypothesis.*

All we can do is try to construct models that enable us to describe and understand reality. There are two tools we can use: logic and observation. Logic is thought and is therefore in the Conceptual Realm; a thought may match reality or it may not. A logical outcome is a correlation identified in a brain. We need to test logical outcomes (arguments) against the Natural Realm to see if they match. Investigating for evidence in the form of repeatable observations is the tool we use to perform this testing. Evidence is the inspector, that's why evidence has supremacy over thought, even over logical thought, even over proof. Some philosophers may claim that you need philosophy to interpret results before you can draw a conclusion but I contend that the philosophizing (thinking) was done earlier when the hypothesis was conceived, and all you are doing *after* the investigation is identifying a match, or not, between the observations and the original concept.

It's important to know where evidence 'stops' because another confusion some theists get into is to blur the distinction between observations and conclusions. They claim that observation and conclusion are *one* procedure and therefore interpretation is involved. This is not correct, they are entirely distinct processes – observation is the collection of data, conclusion is simply seeing if the observations match the original hypothesis – see the example about bird observations given on page 240.

Professional logicians know that logic cannot provide evidence for anything, but keen Christian apologists seem to think that it can.

Remember this: every question that we have succeeded in answering has turned out to have a natural explanation. That makes the 'godunnit' unscientific hypothesis highly improbable. I do not deny the possibility of 'god'; I simply recognize it as merely a hypothesis, like fairies.

IN A NUTSHELL:

1. Evidential information (**Knowns**) do not require believing.
2. Until evidence is forthcoming, the 'god' proposition is merely a guess, a *hypothesis*, not a conclusion.
3. Hypotheses can be believed or disbelieved.
4. The claimed 'immaterial' nature of 'god' (itself an ad hoc fallacy) makes the 'god' hypothesis un-investigable, therefore the existence of a 'god' is an *unscientific hypothesis*.
5. All the questions that have been answered so far have been discovered to have natural explanations. That makes a supernatural deity a *highly improbable unscientific hypothesis*.

Just remember:
It doesn't matter how **strong** your belief is,
It doesn't matter how **many** people share your belief,
It doesn't matter how **long** a belief has been believed.
No amount of belief can turn an idea into a 'concrete fact'.
What turns ideas into 'concrete facts' is...
EVIDENCE

WHAT IS EVIDENCE?

Is it Argument, Experience or Observation?

	Argument	*Experience*	Repeatable Observations
Subjective or Objective?	*Conceptual, Imaginary (Subjective)*	*Subjective includes "Revelations"*	Objective (often made by instruments)
Directly Shareable?	*Only by reportage*	*No - it's personal*	Yes - Look at this!
Repeatable?	*Yes (like stories) but Nullius in Verba*	*No (Can you dream again?)*	Yes Anytime, by anyone, anywhere
Can I do it?	*Yes Anyone can claim to be a 'prophet'*	*Yes Anyone can retell and embellish*	Yes, I can *actually observe* it for myself.
Requires Evaluation?	*Yes*	*Yes, in a tabloid way!*	No. Data is fact
Leads to what?	*An opinion (hypothesis)*	*An opinion*	A Conclusion
Requires Belief?	*Yes*	*Yes*	No
Disputable?	*Yes*	*Yes*	No
Is it Evidence?	*No*	*No*	**YES**

'KNOWNS' VERSUS BELIEFS

	'KNOWNS'	BELIEFS
1.	Supported by *Evidence*	*Supported by Argument NOT evidence*
2.	Evidence is in the form of *Repeatable Observations*	*No repeatable observations, just stories of unique 'miracles'*
3.	Are *Discovered* through *Investigations*, sometimes involving *Experiments*	*Not Investigation based - just repetition or reinterpretation of ancient doctrines*
4.	Do not require active believing	*Chosen attitudes towards propositions that require repeated effort to believe*
5.	Exist Objectively	*Subjective - inside men's heads*
6.	Matched reality before mankind existed	*Began when individuals first imagined them*
7.	Will still match reality after mankind becomes extinct	*End when believers change their minds or die - many ancient beliefs in 'gods' are now dead*
8.	Describe observed data with a single explanation	*Unsubstantiated stories offer many alternative explanations*
9.	Enable predictions which can be investigated for verification	*Predictions are either fantastic or mundane and cannot be verified*
10	Rational and Trustworthy	*Irrational and Untrustworthy*

NB: Hypotheses are informed guesses useful for deciding the direction of scientific investigation. They are not 'true'.

Theories are evidential models of phenomena that have not been falsified and that enable predictions that can be tested.

Repeated observations are facts.

Single observations are just anecdotes.

How do you know when you've got evidence?
It's when other opinions go away.

In the absence of evidence, different people form different opinions.

Evidence is priceless, belief is virtually valueless.

A lack of evidence is also important; for example, there is no evidence that life is a rehearsal for an 'afterlife'.

There is no evidence for mind being separate from brain.

There is no evidence for a 'soul'.

~~~

Seriously... if people have to frighten little children witless in order to get them to believe their claims, what are the chances the claims are even slightly likely to be true?

Paul BROCKLEHURST

5. DEFENDING A BELIEF

As we have seen in the previous chapters, *concepts that are supported by evidence do not need advocating.* They are items of information that are accepted as very probably true, as things that no longer need actively believing or reiterating and consequently don't need arguing about or defending against challenges from disbelievers.

You won't find citizens debating for and against the effect of the force of gravity in the vicinity of Earth; there aren't two contradictory understandings. People will not get arrested for fighting over their different views of the elemental composition of a molecule of water at standard temperature and pressure. It's H_2O, there's no dispute[71]. Since there is no disagreement, the information belongs to everyone; you can't *own* it. So you can't sell your services as a preacher or ask for offerings based on your claimed exclusive access to special knowledge, unlike the clergy who profess to be able to advise you because they have a 'personal relationship with god'.

Beliefs are the opposite of that. They are dubious, contentious, debatable, matters of opinion, causes of disagreement and they *depend upon the power of skilled advocacy (preaching) for persuading the masses.* I accept that I am making the assumption that both contenders in a debate on the existence of 'god' are rational, not deluded and equally well informed, and I realize that is quite a bold assumption to make! If one protagonist is unaware of the evidence about the subject matter, or worse, is unaware of what actually constitutes evidence, then it's *teaching* that is required rather than argument, and that's an entirely different skill set. The difference I am highlighting is revealed by your answers to the following two questions:

1. Do you constantly fear floating away?
2. Do you doubt the beliefs of others?

If you said 'No' to 1 and 'Yes' to 2, you have agreed that 'concrete facts', like gravity, do not require active believing but beliefs are associated with doubt.

DOES GRAVITY NEED BELIEF? NO!   DO BELIEFS BRING DOUBT? YES!

I accept that, in the past, some things, once considered to be 'known', have turned out to be wrong, like geocentricity. That just shows how bad things were before we had access to repeatable observational evidence and it does not alter the way that beliefs and knowns are commonly treated today.

Since beliefs are possibly *false*, a believer can only express an *opinion* towards them. In the absence of evidence, the only thing that proponents of a 'god' can do is to assert their views more emphatically, more vehemently, more passionately, *more argumentatively*. This leads to conflict.

Argument involves emotion and a quarrel often results because what is at risk now is not just an idea. It's a *possession* – a backer has staked *himself*. His reputation and the respect of his peers is under threat. His very status in the community is in peril. An emotional investment as a 'believer' has been made and people tend not to like admitting that they have made bad investments in unsupportable ventures, so it's only human nature to cling to beliefs regardless of their uncertainty. It's no longer about the belief per se, it's now about the ego of the claimant and, consequently, it's perceived as needing defending come hell or high water! No one likes to lose 'face'. No one likes being ridiculed. Nobody wants their social standing diminished. Sadly, I have lost friends through their intransigence about mere hypotheses...

Religions are harmful to relationships. *Needlessly*, since they are non-evidential. We all use evidence to confirm or deny beliefs so evidence *must have supremacy*.

If you are a believer disagreeing with the above analysis ask yourself the following question: 'If I were somehow mistaken about the existence of a god, what would convince me that my belief wasn't reliable?' If *nothing* would that's a sure sign that you've closed off all means of reassessing your beliefs, and where's the virtue in that?

Remember these two things:

- Firstly, when you see an emotional disagreement in progress you are entitled to wonder whether the concept in question is non-evidential. A quarrel is about something obviously contentious or dubious. It's an *issue, not a fact.* It's subject to opinion and is a matter for *belief or disbelief.*
- Secondly, since he/she lacks evidence, the believer has only one course of action available - to resort to ridiculing his opponent's position. It's an easy step from there to insulting the opponent himself (ad hominem). Disagreement turns to conflict.

If he had evidence, a believer would simply be able to point to it and his job would be done. But he doesn't, so he can only deride the opposite position. Deriding 'atheists', his imaginary opposition, is the entire purpose of Andy's book.

Ask yourself, is this difference between beliefs and 'concrete facts' the reason why elementary science books can contain such a lot of information in so few pages? Why they all present the *same* information? Is it because there's nothing very contentious in them? For example, Newton's Laws of Motion, and the evidence for them, can be expressed concisely and they are just as accurate today as they were when Sir Isaac worked them out in 1687. Indeed, they are still used to navigate spacecraft around the solar system. Similarly, The Periodic Table of the Elements imparts information with incredible density.

Elementary Science books only need to be republished when a new syllabus is introduced that reorganizes the order of delivery of the subject matter, or when new printing techniques are developed, as happened when single color and full color illustrations first became available. A new science book is only produced to keep up to date with technology for delivering teaching and learning. There is no point rewriting the same information just for the sake of it because it hardly ever changes! This is why Wikipedia can be regarded as a reliable source for items of unfalsified information. A rogue editor changing the text would look laughably foolish.

Remember the science textbooks you had at school? Apart from looking old-fashioned, there was nothing much wrong with the information in them. OK, you can go back to when Phlogiston was thought to be an explanation for burning, but I'm assuming you weren't at school then! Please note: science textbooks contain two sorts of information – *probable facts*, which can be validated by repeating the experiments described in the books, and *hypotheses* about the frontiers of our knowledge, which await, or are under, investigation.

Unlike factual textbooks, books about belief are often long and rambling and they don't describe any investigations that we can repeat for ourselves, so they can't be verified. The Atheist Who Didn't Exist is a good example: it consists of stories rather than information. We can have one definitive textbook on a science specialism thanks to the presence of evidence, but there is no ultimate explanation due to faith (because of the lack of evidence) so the production line of faith books never stops. Ridiculing the non-belief position is the only thing that theists can do and it's a job that's never finished. Until there is positive evidence for a belief, the arguments will continue because arguments can be strong or weak but never conclusively right or wrong. Conversely, if and when evidence arrives for 'god', arguments will become unnecessary.

For example, theists have many different beliefs about what their god wants. Even though the most popular faith right now (so they claim) happens to be Christianity, its followers can't agree on a whole range of matters, which is why Christians fall into different camps: Catholics and Protestants, Anglicans, Evangelicals, Mormons, Jehovah Witnesses, etc. However, Protestants can't agree among themselves either, so there are many different forms of Protestantism, one of which is Methodism. Do all Methodists agree about their god? Nope, and so it goes on! A Pastor friend of mine describes himself as a Reformed Biblical Evangelist – the only sect that he deems suitable for him! Selection of a faith seems to be driven by dislike of doctrines (ideas) that disagree with your own opinion! It's a negative process rather than positive one, and most people simply abdicate choosing for themselves in favor of meekly going along with the faith of their parents or the society they were born into.

You can even take this issue right down to the level where members of one family probably won't entirely agree on every issue regarding their 'god'. They each have their *own* concept in their heads. Why is this a surprise, though, when there's no reliable means of knowing anything about any 'god', including whether they even exist? Despite this, many Christian authors egotistically think they have a new slant, or a definitive version, that warrants them writing a book, such as trying to make out that 'atheism' is an ideology!

Ask yourself, do we doubt the effect of gravity and disagree about it around the family dinner table? No? Why is that? Is it something to do with evidence?

'We don't know' seems to be anathema to a theist's makeup. In their minds they seem to have no doubt that their understanding of how things work is correct: their godunnit. And they seem to view scientists' admitted ignorance of the answers to 'fundamental questions' as a weakness to exploit. Their desire for certainty means they can scoff at the frontiers of science, the unfinished business. They feel they can criticize and demand high standards of validity, completeness, coherence, accuracy and evidence where science is concerned, *and rightly so*, but one is entitled to ask why they don't apply the same standards to their own propositions? And why do they feel entitled to wriggle and squirm interpreting the heinous stories in the Bible into something that sounds moral when so much of it very clearly is not? Have you actually read the Bible?

Christian theology seems to be about constantly reinterpreting the Bible in an attempt to make it mean what theists would like it to have said! Double standards rule in the apologist world. Christian apologists are well named: they have a busy life trying to excuse the Bible for all its violations of human rights and exemplifications of the victimization of minorities!

~~~

Andy Bannister also mentions beauty, which theists often use as 'proof' of god. They like to ignore tapeworms, stillbirths and malaria parasites and claim that loveliness must 'prove' the existence of an artistic designer/creator. Andy says:

Beauty has to be more than mere opinion; otherwise we're just playing word games. So if beauty isn't a material thing and it isn't a subjective, personal, psychological projection, what is it?
(my underlining)

Firstly, *'has to be'*? Who says what *has* to be? And I thought Andy *loved* playing word games, didn't you? Isn't The Atheist Who Didn't Exist one long *opinionated word game?*

Secondly, please notice that Andy is asking a *question, 'What is it'?* (beauty) He is *not* providing an answer. Many theists seem to think that questioning our lack of understanding is equivalent to proving their 'god' proposition to be true! *It's not.* Would you accept a claim that rainbows look beautiful

158

because leprechauns ('god' in Andy's mind) made them that way? No! Not only because no one believes in leprechauns but also because, even if they did exist, the beauty of a rainbow is in no way *explained* by little green-clad Irishmen *or for that matter any unseen deity.* What is needed is an *explanatory mechanism* for the cause of rainbows, and science has given us that – it's the refraction of sunlight through raindrops. No 'god' required. Science postulates a *process*; religion postulates a *being.* One *tests* its postulations for a match with evidence, the other *doesn't do testing.*

Thirdly, yes, beauty has long been a qualitative concept residing in the eye of the beholder but science is now beginning to get to grips with it. Facial recognition systems can already identify faces with such stunning accuracy that they can identify known criminals as they *enter a shop,* and they are on the brink of rating faces for 'beauty'. Recent software has produced average faces for females in forty-one countries! See here http://tinyurl.com/hub6jz6

Beauty is about symmetry, contrast, composition, color co-ordination and proportion, features that are beginning to be quantified. Algorithms are probably being written right now… Ok, humans are programming them currently, but the development of computer learning possibly means that, soon, our input will be unnecessary. In 2016, Google's computer,

Deepmind, taught itself to beat the best human champions at Go[72]. Its programmers do not know how it did it! Since then, a computer has beaten four professional poker players. They are now incorporating imagination! Theists are being *stuffed* by Artificial Intelligence!

Faith is the denial of observation so that belief can be preserved.'
Tim MINCHEN

Atheists 'Have Nothing to Die For... We Have Everything to Live For'
Ricky GERVAIS

Faith is what credulity becomes when it finally achieves escape velocity from the constraints of human discourse.
Sam HARRIS

SUMMARY OF CHAPTER 5

- Conceptualizing (thinking) is the domain of philosophy.
- There is no automatic correspondence between concepts (thoughts) and reality.
- Investigating concepts for correspondence with reality is the purview of science.
- Evidence for distinguishing between the real and the unreal comes from the Natural Realm in the form of shareable, repeatable observations of reality.
- Some concepts are intended to be fictitious, (e.g. fairytales).
- Some concepts are intended to deceive, (e.g. man-made optical illusions).
- Some concepts are intended to be hypothetical, (especially concerning the 'immaterial').
- Some hypotheses are testable and can turn out to match reality. They get converted to conclusions if they are confirmed by observations. They are material and, once concluded, become 'knowns', which do not require active belief unless challenged by new evidence.
- Some hypotheses are untestable and doomed to remain merely concepts. These are the non-evidential immaterial propositions. They require belief. They need defending.
- When confronted by ignorance, an argument may need resolving not by arguing, but by teaching, and the first thing that might have to be taught is how to recognize evidence...

Disagreements between one faith-based view and another are almost inevitable and can cause great conflicts because you can't beat one faith claim with another faith claim. Think what this means. When you hear an argument in progress you can be pretty sure that the subject in question is *not* a 'concrete fact'. It's just a proposition, a hypothesis, merely a belief or opinion. Arguments cannot be either true or false; they can only be strong or weak opinions. Remember, argument stops when evidence is produced. The need for belief also stops when evidence is produced.

Why are believers so easily offended? Here's my hypothesis: Beliefs, being merely *personal* attitudes (opinions) towards propositions, can only be defended emotionally, which requires investment of one's ego. So one takes possession of a belief and to have it challenged is to risk losing status in the social hierarchy, hence it's a tender area. Ownership exposes one to possible personal loss, which is never enjoyable.

Information that is not doubtful, however, like the effect of gravity, is COMMON knowledge and not a subject for dispute, therefore no one needs to argue about it or feel offended if it's questioned. (In fact, a gravity questioner would be universally thought to be mad.) There is no individual ownership of common knowledge and so no risk of personal loss.

162

Beliefs, however, are dubious, disputable and need to be protected. Some faiths enforce protection with severe punishments for challenging their doctrines. They enact bogus crimes of heresy, blasphemy, apostasy, etc. Sanctions even include execution. Ask yourself, isn't that a clue about their unjustifiability?

Let's take a closer look at gravity as an example of a 'concrete fact' The fine details about what gravity actually *is* are still under investigation - gravity waves in the space-time continuum were discovered recently, will it be particulate 'gravitons' next? But the *effects* of gravity are not in dispute; it behaves like a force of attraction between masses that is proportional to the sizes of the masses and that diminishes in relation to the square of the distance. We can model this effect mathematically. Nobody doubts what will happen if they jump off a cliff. Beliefs, however, have a different level of credibility – we all know this because everyone doubts the beliefs of others. We even doubt our own beliefs sometimes. Doubt is the bedfellow of belief but an abomination to what the Stanford Encyclopedia of Philosophy refers to as 'concrete facts' (knowns). A belief is just a chosen opinion about the unknown, that's the point I am trying to make in this book.

6. HOW SCIENCE WORKS

Since many theists tend to regard science as the enemy, we obviously need to help them to grasp what science is actually about. It's the lack of understanding of scientific method that leads people to think they can make a case for a magic (godly) explanation for anything and everything. Yes, oddly, those who often wrongly accuse scientists of claiming to explain everything and failing actually DO claim to have an explanation themselves (with no evidence)! Hypocrisy or what! There follows my attempt to explain how science works.

Discovery usually starts with conceptualizing a likely explanation for a question (but see item 10 later). Nobody likes to admit they don't know, so we can't face a question for long without guessing possible answers for it. Until it has been tested, there is a risk that people will decide for themselves that this guess is correct, without waiting for justification. This happens a lot! It's rather like negative campaigning in an election – an allegation that lacks evidence can often ruin a candidate's reputation just as much as a legal conviction can.

So we think up a hypothesis that may provide an answer to some puzzle that we would like solved. Hypotheses are concepts. There is no limit to conceptualizing - some concepts are purely fictitious - such as Humpty Dumpty, so hypotheses

164

have to be sorted into reasonable and unreasonable propositions. We don't bother to investigate unreasonable propositions – we have better things to do!

If we think it is a reasonable one, we test a hypothesis to see whether whatever it predicts matches reality by investigating for evidence in the form of repeatable observations.

The observations from reality are compared with the hypothesis to see whether there is a match or not. If the observations match the prediction, they turn the hypothesis into a conclusion - a piece of real information: a 'known'. Some hypotheses are not matched by observations, so they remain hypotheses until they *do* get confirmed, if ever.

Once confirmed by observations, it means a number of things:

1. The hypothesis (Concept) has become the answer to a question – it is now a *Scientific Conclusion*.

2. Conclusions usually inspire more questions leading to further hypotheses that may, in turn, be investigated.

3. Sometimes conclusions fit together to explain complex phenomena so we can assemble them into a Theory. Theories enable predictions that can be tested further to add

another layer of confirmation or even, possibly, to improve the previous conclusion.

4. Becoming a conclusion doesn't terminate conceptualizing - even though we have proven the feasibility of the jet engine concept, we can still conceptualize jet engines. Concepts can be converted from hypotheses to conclusions, but nothing ever leaves the Conceptual Realm. We can conceive of trees even though we know them to be real phenomena. We can conceive of Humpty Dumpty although we know him to be fiction. There is no limit to conceptualizing.

5. A concept that fails to match observations languishes in the Conceptual Realm. Some concepts (hypotheses) are currently awaiting investigation; they remain merely concepts for the time being. Somebody needs to do some research!

6. Other hypotheses are under investigation but the observations are not in yet. They also remain hypotheses for the time being. Ambient temperature superconductors are in this category. We can imagine them; we just haven't succeeded in making them yet.

7. Some concepts (hypotheses) are uninvestigable, so they may remain merely concepts forever or, at least, until we develop new technologies that enable us to investigate them.

A 'Supernatural Creator Deity' is in this category. In fact, it has been 'protected' from investigation by postulating its 'immateriality' - that is an ad hoc fallacy - a hypothesis intended to prevent another hypothesis from being falsified.

8. A conclusion does not need active believing. It's regarded as a 'known', a THING THAT IS, to use Andy's expression. We behave as though conclusions are 'true' right up until they are falsified. We do not have to constantly affirm belief in 'knowns' because they do not attract doubt. Unless you doubt what will happen if you jump off a roof, that is.

9. Believing is the preserve of hypotheses - things for which we have no evidence. It is necessary to choose to believe in propositions because they have a high possibility of being false, unlike 'knowns'. Feel free to believe in the Loch Ness Monster if you wish. On the other hand, unfalsified information supported by observations doesn't need any attention from the activity of believing - it has achieved the status of 'known'.

10. Sometimes it's the other way round - an unexpected observation is detected and we have to conceptualize a possible explanation for it afterwards; the planet Neptune was discovered after noticing perturbations in the orbit of Uranus.

11. Despite the evidence of a vast mountain of successfully explained phenomena that were once mysterious, some

people deny that this scientific method of discovering information is the only effective one, and plump for an emotional affinity to a non-evidential hypothesis, a 'gut-feeling' or 'act of faith'.

So, evidence in the form of repeatable observations is what turns hypotheses (challengeable propositions) into conclusions (unfalsified 'knowns'). Nothing else.

Our understanding of the effect of gravity fits into this description. Repeated measurements have confirmed Newton's Laws of Motion countless times. Scientists don't say that they have been proven; we use the term 'currently unfalsified' because it is unwise to be dogmatically certain. Theists have a different attitude towards this! Science is reasonable uncertainty; religion is unreasonable certainty.

In fact, although Newton's 'Laws' model nature accurately enough to navigate around the solar system (except near Mercury) we now know that, at close to light speed, or over interstellar distances, Einstein's Theory of Relativity is better.

Now, I know I'm going to be challenged on the grounds that Science rests on an assumption: the assumption of materialism (that there is nothing supernatural). So, ok, it's true that the materialism concept cannot be proven logically without getting into circular arguments, but it is thoroughly evidential, has never been falsified and has enabled the construction of many theories that explain much of the behavior of the universe and everything in it. Meanwhile, there is no evidence at all for anything 'supernatural'. This is simply a case of observation trumping thoughts. Ok, we can't *think* of a way to validate the assumption of materialism but that doesn't mean it's not a useful foundation for building an understanding of reality on. Thought is thought, so a failed thought is only a failed thought. Materialism *hasn't* failed.

Yes, there are some remaining unknowns, but to question materialism is to cast doubt on every aspect of modern life that has spun-off from science. That would include all our means of transport (apart from walking), medical treatments and the very computer that I am writing this book on. Ask yourself, is it sensible to throw everything out in favor of a hypothetical 'immaterial god' in an 'immaterial realm' and for religious doctrines that have given us nothing but strife? What if I reverse the challenge and point out that philosophy rests on concepts that are unverifiable too? Logic makes the assumption of rationality and order. Just because our brains have evolved to seek explanations in the form of patterns, that doesn't mean that nature must be regular. In fact Quantum Theory is very counter intuitive – it breaks the patterns of classical physics.

SUMMARY OF CHAPTER 6

Remember, in Science:

- We are only making MODELS of reality.
- We base our conclusions on evidence in the form of shareable, repeatable observations.
- We have discovered nothing absolute so it seems likely there are no absolute grand universal truths; truth is conceptual or social. The best we can do in reality is to get a high probability of accuracy and wait to see if our understanding ever gets falsified.
- Everything is relative to something else - to time, temperature, location, velocity, scale, medium, pressure, or even to how the observations are made.
- Proof doesn't exist except in the Conceptual Realm (e.g. in math and logic), so it's subordinate to evidence.
- *Science is reasonable uncertainty; religion is unreasonable certainty.* (That can't be said too often!)

Alternatively, we can *imagine* that choosing to believe in a 'god' has some objective importance greater than deciding trivialities such as how much sugar to put in coffee. Then we can pin 'explanations' for the mysteries of the universe on to this hypothetical non-evidential deity. At that point we can egotistically imagine that we are special people bound for an afterlife of bliss who are entitled to inflict our beliefs upon others, especially children, and allow some fellow believers to become radicalized for the mission of spreading our belief system to all and sundry on pain of death. Ask yourself, who would want that?

So, science makes models and tests them for a match with reality. We base our understanding on the models that match most accurately, until they are falsified by new observations, which may never happen. We have found no absolute truth in the Natural Realm.

THE 'GOD-SHAPED HOLE'

Why do a few scientists (7% of the American Academy for the Advancement of Science) persist in believing in a god then? On the face of it, this is perplexing but there is an evolutionary explanation. The environment is full of threats, so we are adapted to fear the unknown – we live longer to breed more if we jump away from a snake even if we subsequently discover it was just a stick. It's also an advantage to learn about our environment, to distinguish the poisonous snakes from the harmless ones that we might be able to eat. So we have evolved curiosity: a thirst for learning. Knowing is comforting: ignorance is *not* bliss! On the contrary, *not knowing* is fraught with doubt and worry that disturbs our sleep at night. So we

171

are born with a 'god-shaped hole', a yearning for explanations so strong that we are prepared to satisfy that desire by *inventing* solutions in the absence of actual answers. Our brains are adapted to make hasty assumptions, to jump to conclusions. It's safer even though it is irrational. The easiest closure to a puzzle that is disturbing us is always Godunnit. Even scientists can fall into this trap. Remember, we need evidence *for* a god; She's not a sticking plaster to patch over the worrisome blanks in our understanding.

'Anything that's truly real can stand up to scrutiny.' Science adjusts its views based on what is observed.'

Carl SAGAN

7. MORALITY

I'm afraid that the second part of Andy's Chapter 2 is based on another blatantly unevidenced assumption, another mere hypothesis: *that morality is a gift from 'god'*. Honestly, it's difficult to see how a 'god' who is described as genocidal, if the Bible is anything to go by, a 'god' who favors misogyny, homophobia, the raping of daughters and the stoning of naughty sons might be able to teach us anything about morals! (Yes, I know that Christians will try to wriggle their way out of those references.) Anybody who has actually read the Bible will know that, on balance, the benevolent advice it contains is heavily out-weighed by the malice it exemplifies.

It's also difficult to see how a non-evidential, 'immaterial' 'god' might be able to do *anything at all* for us material human beings on our material planet, in the material galaxy, in the material universe, unless She materializes (becomes matter, i.e. *real*), comes off Her hypothetical sky throne and down from Her hypothetical 'heaven'. And what method would She use to deliver Her morality to us? Telegram? Fax? Texting? Whatsapp? Snapchat? 'Revelation'? Oh, yes, stone tablets! Or buried golden plates if you subscribe to Mormonism! In other words, *by means of the technology available at the time the 'scripture' was written!* Ask yourself, isn't this consistent with the suggestion that *men* wrote those texts?

Theists don't help us here because, not only do they disagree about which religious morality is the 'correct' one, they don't offer any explanation for how their pet *'immaterial'* deity might have been able to influence our *material* universe (with Her ghostly hand?) in the 13.8 billion years since it probably began to exist, *nor* any evidence for occasions on which Her moral influence has actually been wielded for the benefit of us humans, 'Her children' supposedly. On the contrary, She is conspicuously absent at times of disaster!

Furthermore, as well as studiously ignoring their 'god's' countless malicious interventions in human affairs (reported in their own 'scriptures') and lack of humane interventions,

174

many Christians overlook the often sadistic sanctions applied by the earthly 'representatives' of 'god' to those who commit doctrinal violations such as 'heresy', 'blasphemy' and 'apostasy', or even 'witchiness'. Meanwhile, the evidence for *no* benevolent 'godly' salvation arrives daily in the form of news of global disasters ('Acts of God' in insurance terminology – insurers truly understand Her heartless uncaring nature!) and religiously inspired terrorist atrocities. The world is in such a state we would be justified in wondering whether 'god' is 'evil'!

Andy quotes the famous philosopher, Nietzsche, who said,

"When one gives up the Christian faith, one pulls the right to Christian morality out from under one's feet."

That's a selected quote: a 'cherry pick'. Nietzsche was well aware that there are *other moralities*, including Islamic morality and Jewish morality because he wrote about them both, so he must have recognized that *Christians have no right to claim exclusive ownership of morality*. This is what Wikipedia has to say:

"In Ecce Homo, Nietzsche called the establishment of moral systems based on a dichotomy of good and evil a 'calamitous error', and wished to initiate a re-evaluation of the values of the Judeo-Christian world. He indicates his desire to bring about a new, more naturalistic source of value in the vital impulses of life itself."

"A new, more naturalistic source of value in the vital impulses of life itself"? (my question mark) Sounds like Nietzsche was proposing *evolved* morality to me!

Meanwhile, the fact is there are different moralities, some associated with different religious doctrines, which change over time and which originate *in populations in different geographical locations.* Ask yourself, isn't that a clue to the human fabrication of morals? Also, anyone who has lived a long life will have seen how moral attitudes can change, which surely reveals the man-made nature of morality.

Here's an example: when I was a teenager, the expectation was for young men to 'sow their wild oats' with little concern for the consequences to a girl. Boys were depicted as incorrigibly irresponsible in an increasingly permissive society. Girls in short skirts were deemed to be 'asking for it'. Since then, the availability of reliable contraception and feminism have, in their different ways, altered sexual attitudes in Western societies. Now the sexes are pretty much equal, making the sex act a matter of mutual consent and shared responsibility. This change has not occurred in some Islamic cultures where females are still burdened with being the custodians of copulation and are regarded as culpable

176

temptresses for the uncontrollable lust of males. Hence the all-enveloping black burqa – a portable woman cage, and stoning to death for adultery. That is a different moral climate.

So, not only can morality change over time, but also it can vary between different geographical locations. Actually, since cheap air travel, the locations have become mingled and several different cultures can share a city, neighborhood by neighborhood. Some cities have problems as a result of the clash of moralities.

Surely, before postulating that She can bestow morality, shouldn't we establish that 'god' actually exists? Don't we need to *discover* Her first? What is the point of piling hypothesis upon hypothesis? There can be no godly moral imperative if there is no god (see Chapter 8). In any case, the godly moral command notion falls foul of the Euthyphro problem[73]...

Suggesting that a hypothetical being can bestow morals on us and that without belief in Her we would all be rampaging rapists, arsonists, thieves and murderers is just compounding the felony of hypothesizing. Besides that, *it's bloody insulting!* Especially as theists haven't even agreed amongst themselves which hypothetical deity's morality is the 'true' one! Some Christians will claim that there is just one true 'god' and the different religions are just different ways of worshipping Her. I ask them, "Why has the one true 'god' given such a different moral message to Muslims then?"

And, surely, following a doctrine under threat of eternal torture in 'Hell' is *not* exercising morality; it's succumbing to intimidation by the watchful eye of the 'Holy Closed Circuit Television'! Similarly, being 'good' in order to 'go to heaven' is not moral; it's accepting a bribe! So many religions, each with their own version of 'morality', they can't all be right, but they *can* all be wrong!

178

So, from where might morality originate, if not from Her? Well, there is increasing evidence, from several different strands of investigation, showing that morality is not sourced from any religion but comes from nature. Here are four examples:

- Infant studies: Religious morality can only be imparted by means of language and yet our pre-lingual infants exhibit an understanding of pro-social behaviors such as compassion, co-operation, fairness and reciprocity. See here: http://tinyurl.com/keuokp5

  To my shame, the young me ducked out of a relationship with a single mother because her unspeaking toddler (not my child) started to bring my shoes to help me dress, to show helpful behavior. She was so cute, but I wasn't ready for fatherhood.

- Anthropology: All human communities, *irrespective of their local religion* exhibit the 'moral universals' of prohibiting murder and theft.

- Animal Behavior Studies: Many non-human social animals possess an early morality to varying degrees. Monkeys, apes, elephants, dogs and dolphins display some understanding of reciprocity, fairness, nurturing and compassion. Bonobo chimpanzees will console losers (http://tinyurl.com/aqykq9f); swans will feed fish (http://tinyurl.com/ht228wt); parental orang-utans will raise

179

tiger cubs (http://tinyurl.com/glycg5g); dogs will rescue injured dogs (http://tinyurl.com/jco62z6).

• Criminology: There is a *negative* link between religiosity and crime. More religion correlates with more crime, i.e. *lower* morality! See here: http://tinyurl.com/hmrero4

All of this points to the fact that morality has evolved. Looking after each other benefits a social species by making peaceful, safe, communal conditions that facilitate the successful nurturing of vulnerable young. It enables the adults to spend time parenting and it fosters well-being so the herd may grow in numbers – that's success.

Cooperation works *within* a clan but, naturally, competition for resources will occur *between* groups so we need an aggressive side to defend our territory and its resources against rivals. In evolutionary terms, protecting one's kin from the threat of an out-group is very moral behavior.

Religions take advantage of our evolved tendency to build such coherent peaceable communities. They parasitize on our behavioral adaptation to foster well-being within a tribe. Perhaps if there was just one religion, all would be congenial but, sadly, there are several different faiths and that brings the competitive animosity between rival tribes into play. This may not have been too much of a problem when the population was so small that we rarely encountered competing cults, but we have the jumbo jet now. Cheap transport has opened the door to clashes between different religious societies who can now live cheek by jowl. We are currently seeing cultural strife in Germany between newly immigrant, sexually repressed young Muslim men and young free-thinking Western females: a collision between two very different expectations of how women should be treated.

Yes, all societies have had some psychopaths and yes, we have had to respond to attacks by turning our normally benign nature into an aggressive one, which shows that morality is expedient not absolute, but the fact that there are over seven billion of us is a clue to the overall success of our inherited strategy for mainly co-operative, socially benevolent, behavior. So, it's a mistake to assume that morality is fixed: that's the sort of unforgiving attitude that leads to inhumane sanctions dating back to the early days of civilisation, and it's also not a good idea to generalise from a few deviant outliers to the entire population.

Who is claiming that a single perfect practical solution for communal living has evolved? Not me. The opposite is the case – we have evolved a diversity of behavioral responses to situations, some of which suit current conditions more than others. But conditions can change and we may benefit from more, or less, aggression in the future. And who says that morality has stopped evolving? Not me. We can already see a range of different human moralities from peaceful, tolerant secular societies like in Denmark, to cruel, intolerant religious societies like in Saudi Arabia where women are not even permitted to drive a car.

So morality is at least partly contingent – even murder is appropriate to protect one's family if their lives are being threatened. Yes, we can *conceive* of an 'absolute morality' but the Conceptual Realm is not reality (a synonym for 'conceptual' is 'imaginary'). Right now, we need to realize that basing disagreement on *non-evidential gods* is one cause of conflict that we could well do without. There are enough real differences to fall out over.

Presumably, Andy claims that only his *Christian* 'god' is the source of morality, not any other 'gods' because *they* are all false! What about secularists? Can't we be moral? No? How rude! If you read it thoroughly you will find the Bible is not exactly a good moral compass and it claims that 'god' *created* 'evil'! Why would a 'good god' do that? And why did an eternal 'god' wait about 13.8 billion years from when She created the universe, right up until about 2000 years ago (at least 198,000 years *after* Homo sapiens first appeared, so far as we know) before She felt it necessary to provide Her so-called guidance for moral behavior? Ask yourself that...

Hasn't Andy seen the data that correlates crime and corruption with high religiosity[74]? Doesn't he know that walls have had to be constructed in highly religious cities like Belfast and Jerusalem to keep the supporters of different faiths/sects apart in an attempt to prevent them from killing each other[75]? Who are the most barbaric people today? Non-believers or believers? Do a bit of research...

MILITANT BELIEVERS   'MILITANT ATHEIST'

Yes, in highly secular communities, behaviors are matters of individual guided opinion. Almost without exception, humans have disgust for brutality and are, by and large, adapted to cooperate, to nurture, to empathize, but there are circumstances in which we form the view that it is expedient to act against our 'programming'. Killing is *not* absolutely wrong; killing a person who is trying to kill the vulnerable may *save* lives. Hopefully we will not be put in this dilemma, but few would argue that the rescue of a child that involves killing the child's would-be murderer is inappropriate.

So, don't judge the entire herd by the behavior of an outlier (sociopath) who may have a psychological defect. I'm not a psychologist, but I understand that diagnoses have historically been descriptions of behaviors rather than actual identifications of physical, metabolic or physiological defects, although that may be changing with modern neurological and genome reading techniques. Some psychological disorders are being discovered to be due to genetic causes. See here - http://tinyurl.com/m6qqg8n

Morality has its roots in empathy, which is the tendency to link with one another. Our brains have 'mirror neurons[77]' which fire when we observe others performing an action in the same way as if we were doing it ourselves. Empathy is the reason that yawning and scratching are contagious. Imagining ourselves to be in a skilled person's shoes is how we learn. We observe them and mimic their behavior and it's not just us: many animals learn by mimicking too, the house sparrows in my garden have copied the blue tits' way of eating peanuts from the bird feeder. I'm a copyist as well. I learned to play the guitar by watching the lead guitarist in our local band. We are apes; we do aping. It's also how we coach - we can often see where a player is going wrong even if we are incapable of his level of performance ourselves.

When nonbelievers like me talk about being 'good without god' we occasionally get theists accuse us of setting ourselves up as superior to 'god' and the next thing we're told is that we need some humility! Well, that insult is only valid if there *is* a 'god'. So, until the existence of a 'god' has been demonstrated beyond doubt, we are entitled to take that allegation as merely rhetoric intended to defend a doctrine (idea), or to insult non-believers. Ask yourself, how humble is the Christian accuser, with his belief in being specially chosen for an afterlife of eternal bliss? Isn't this hypocrisy?

Then in his attempt to denigrate 'atheism' (the ideology that doesn't exist), Andy claims that eugenics and social Darwinism[78] are *'atheist'* ideas! I quote:

And, of course, what about bad atheist ideas? What about eugenics, Social Darwinism, and that ridiculous bus?

Throughout his book, Andy persists in making the mistake of assuming that 'atheism' is an ideology with values, principles and policies. I ask you, who is on the committee that formulates 'atheist' doctrines, the 'atheist' equivalent to the Council of Nicaea, or the Westminster Assembly, or the General Synod, or The Vatican Council? Come to that, where is the hierarchical 'atheist' organization based - where are the 'sacred' headquarters of 'Atheism'? Who is the Archbishop of 'Atheism'? Who is my 'atheist' parish priest? Where is my local 'atheist' church? What are my 'atheist Commandments'? Where is my 'atheist' bible? What are my 'atheist' dietary taboos? Should I not cut my hair and grow a beard? How many non-believers even know what 'social Darwinism' is? Of course, without incorrectly assuming that 'atheism' is like a religion, theists would have no 'atheists' to denigrate and Andy would have had *no book to write!*

The truth is that there is no 'atheist' committee formulating a policy of whether to pursue eugenics or social Darwinism or not, and 'that ridiculous bus' was the initiative of a single benefactor and some advisors. There are *no* 'atheist' policy makers to decide whether to introduce 'social Darwinism' even if it was desirable, which it is not. Survival of the fittest may come into play in the relatively rare occasions of environmental stress in nature, but it does not facilitate the success of a community of social animals during stable habitat conditions like those that humanity has experienced in recorded history. 'Social Darwinism' would be like imposing

186

wartime attitudes on a peacetime society or inflicting the 'rule of the jungle' on a farm! Such nonsense.

Then there are the Christian accusations that 'atheists' are immoral god-haters who are purposeless and have nothing to live for. How people *who don't believe in an afterlife* can be accused of 'having nothing to live for' beats me! Surely, in the absence of an 'afterlife', *real* life is *all* there is to live for! That's just typically contorted theistic thinking. Without the promise of martyrdom and an expedited heavenly meeting with a non-evidential god, suicide bombing would be revealed as *genuinely purposeless*, wouldn't it? And Christian 'morality', is anything but 'good', being based on threats of 'hell', promises of 'heaven' and a get-out clause of 'forgiveness' that enables any 'sinner' to obtain 'salvation' by submitting to the 'Hail Marys' prescribed by the priest. This style of thinking removes responsibility for actions in life and condones atrocities committed in 'The Name of the Lord'. How moral is that?

The threat, "You are going to Hell", comes into the same category. 'Hell' is only for those who believe in it: that doesn't include 'atheists'! My advice is to beware of someone who threatens you while simultaneously claiming to look after you and love you, especially if they ask for money. That's extortion: a gangster protection racket! It's *illegal*.

Don't you just love the superior, high moral tone, 'holier than thou' attitude paraded by some Christians? Especially when it comes from groups whose fundamentalist or clerical wings currently (or historically) victimize women, ostracize homosexuals, sexually abuse children, burn 'witches', imprison 'heretics' and 'blasphemers' or, in the case of recent Islamic fundamentalists, go on shooting sprees and suicide bombing missions shouting 'Allahu akbar'!

Do you know the expression 'putting the cart before the horse'? The fact that we don't have any evidence for a 'god' yet is, let's face it, a major problem for discovering Her morals! Among other things, it means that 'god' can't be *definitely* the source of morality. The most She can be is *hypothetically* (i.e. *guessed* to be) the source of morality. Why aren't believers challenged on this more often?

Religious moralities are all different, but they're all obsessed with sex! Islam relieves its men of responsibility for their 'uncontrollable lust' by restricting the freedom and dress of women, thereby shifting the burden of sexual morality onto females who are very much the subordinate sex in devout Islamic culture. Orthodox Jews insist on cutting the tips off their newborn baby boys' penises (with sometimes deadly results[79]). It seems that being created in god's image wasn't quite perfect enough in that department! Roman Catholicism is against contraception because it regards breeding, along with an insistence that all babies should be brought up *in the faith*, as one of the means of spreading its doctrine and taking over the world! Isn't that a clue? Religions are about *control*.

Virginity is a recurring theme, although even the more liberal Christian societies cannot agree on the age of consent to sex, which is fifteen in France and sixteen in the United Kingdom. Aren't those differences and the sex obsession another clue? Ask yourself, what creature has a sexual fixation and can compose 'moral' laws and a code of ethical behavior in written form? Who do you think made this stuff up?

For non-believers, behaviors are matters of guided opinion. We are adapted to cooperate, to nurture, to empathize, etc, but there may be circumstances in which we form the opinion that it is expedient to act against our programming. (See example of justified killing above)

189

As for the origin of morality, well, some animals have a rudimentary form of it. We are at least partially *programmed* (i.e. we have evolved) to behave the way we do. Ancient animals are much more prone to eating their own eggs than more recently evolved ones. We can see a progression in 'moralities' as creatures become more 'sophisticated' and therefore it becomes more costly, in terms of energy expenditure (calories), to reproduce. The living species can be observed for their behaviors, while the fossil record can indicate their place in the succession of life on Earth.

There are 'pillars' of morality including –

- EMPATHY is the tendency to link with another. It's what we do when we watch a movie and identify with the hero. It's how we learn - we observe someone else and copy him or her. It's how we coach - we can often see where a player is going wrong even if we are incapable of performing at his standard ourselves.
- RECIPROCITY is an understanding of sharing. It can even be delayed gratification or a promise for the future.
- FAIRNESS is the 'golden rule' of 'Do As You Would Be Done By'.

Many animals share those tendencies with us. What's that? You want evidence? Good for you! Here it is:

Bonobo chimpanzees have a quite well developed morality and they're not the only species, see here:

http://tinyurl.com/jmdre93
http://tinyurl.com/jnatg64

Social animals, like Bonobos and ourselves, have evolved *compliance*. That is, we are subject to peer pressure; we want to fit in. It makes for a peaceful community. Compliance means that a few of us, after training by simply growing up in the community and observing what is acceptable behavior and what is not, can step up to act as leaders, while a majority of us are prepared to adopt a deferential role. This tendency to be led, to 'worship' a boss, to be subservient to an organizer is at least part of the inspiration behind the fabrication of religions. Clever faith leaders spotted an opportunity!

Such 'Follow-my-leader' behavior is not peculiar to humans; it has evolved in many social animals and, overall, it makes a species more successful. Is the following clip an example of animal 'worship' of a 'god'? http://tinyurl.com/htg6znw Has religion 'surfed' on the wave of this evolved adaptation and tuned it to specifically benefit the leaders of the religion?

Neurological investigations have shown that the same brain areas 'light up' when we observe someone suffering from an

191

injury as when we experience that injury ourselves. Being able to imagine another's pain is a deterrent to deliberately harming someone – it works on an individual level. So we have an innate inclination to be kind to other individuals *and* to co-operate in a group. Yes, these tendencies can be consciously over-ridden but, being 'hard-wired' characteristics developed during infancy in the growing brain, they at least have to be taken into account at the first response level.

Of course, there is a spectrum of severity of antisocial behaviors: a moral landscape with hard regions and soft ones. For example, inconsiderate queuing - pushing others out of the way to get something for oneself, is regarded as a selfish act but not a crime, while at the other end of the range, it has been agreed that raping a child is a serious offence. This can be explained in evolutionary terms as follows: queue jumping is just relatively harmless competition within a species, which produces more assertive leaders and therefore benefits the species at the low cost of a few disgruntled individuals, but child raping has no benefit to the species, is empathically offensive and risks severe retribution by members of the baby's family and society at large. Morality is partly situational and consequential. Given an odious dilemma, we might have to choose the least evolutionarily *unacceptable* option.

Where we are often mistaken in discussing morality is in

looking at specific individual acts rather than considering how the outcome affects the overall population. It is a propensity of humans to be self-centered and to look at everything from a personal viewpoint. This is exemplified in Biblical claims that 'god' created everything *for us*. Thinking in this egocentric manner causes us to imagine that we are important, that there are *absolute* moral truths and that we can assume authority for making value judgments about whether or not the standards are being violated by another person or by a nation.

We should be thinking of populations not individual actions. There is no evidence for absoluteness but murder is wrong in general because it reduces the population unnecessarily. It is usually a shot in the foot but, occasionally, murder is right - shoot the school gunman - better to kill one maniac than to allow him to kill many children. Morality is often contingent and not absolute.

In general, humans (and many other social species) behave very benignly towards each other. Such 'good' behavior makes for relatively peaceful communities, which are ideal conditions for reproduction and the rearing of young. We have a hierarchical organization with a leader to keep order and we have a territory, which we protect to sustain us. This works so well that we have succeeded in occupying all of the habitable environments on our planet and have amassed a huge population: evolutionary explanations fit these facts very well. Evolved morality has been a huge success for social animals over many eons, as vast herds of zebra and flocks of starlings testify. Christians claiming to have introduced morality when animals possessed it even before humans evolved and well before Jesus allegedly existed, is nothing less than theft!

Yes, there are a few human psychopaths, but they are in a small minority and they have not impeded the success of our species greatly. Turn your telescopes round and stop focusing on individuals. Yes, there have been occasions when societies have become destructive (often inspired or perpetuated by beliefs in different 'gods') but even these horrendous events are small variations in the overall trend of success. Morality has evolved to be advantageous for humanity in general, despite some specific tragic events affecting individuals or nations at times throughout history. Sam Harris does a very good analysis of moral values here: http://tinyurl.com/op26xu5

One bone of contention that arises in the discussion of morality is the theist's claim that "You can't get an ought from an is". They are attempting to argue that there is no way to progress from observations of behavior to moral intentions. In one sense they are right. Intentions are conceptual (imaginary) while observations actually exist in nature. There is no obvious crossover mechanism between the Natural Realm and the Conceptual Realm. So, "You can't get an ought from an is" sounds like a category error statement like "You can't get a fairy from a banana". They are misled into this view by Hume:

"The Scottish philosopher Hume found that there seems to be a significant difference between positive statements (about what is) and prescriptive or normative statements (about what ought to be), and that it is not obvious how one can coherently move from descriptive statements to prescriptive ones." (Wikipedia)

Well, it may not have been obvious to Hume, but, growing up in a family with a developing brain enables us to recognize which behaviors are deemed acceptable and we form our concepts of what we 'ought' to do by watching others, by observing the 'is' of how older family members behave. Neuroscience offers a hypothetical explanation for the mechanism by which we adopt our morality: we know that human brains are incompletely developed when newly born and many neural connections are added in the spurt of early growth. Since an infant is exposed to society during that period, it is possible that the very architecture of the added connections reflects the objective morality of its group – we are 'hardwired' to become socialized and, as we are learning to speak our first language, we are also learning moral behavior.

195

Children observe themselves being cared for so they grow up to care for others in their turn. This explanation is consistent with the 'damaged personality' that we observe in those raised under poor nurturing circumstances. This is not a Biblically imposed or taught morality, it is an objective morality, observed in life by an infant with a growing brain adapted to become socialized with the help of those mirror neurons. It's a transition from an 'is' to an 'ought'.

Of course, even if we have the moral brain of one brought up in well-socialized circles, we can still break out of our programming and make extreme choices when required; we would kill to protect the vulnerable from a murderous threat.

It helps to think of morality as being like jazz music: it has a backing track of acceptable behavior over which a tune can be played. Much of the time, the tune is recognizable as a familiar song but then the lead instrument goes off in an exciting improvised flight of fancy. The chord sequence of objective morality is going, "Don't kill, don't kill, don't kill" repeatedly but, on top, the trumpet of subjective morality is saying, "I can go anywhere and do what I want!" This tension leads to a community that is predominantly stable and peaceful, but has occasional outbursts of revolutionary or anti-social behavior.

The fact is, with the spread of democracy and globalism, there has been an enormous reduction in conflict and in malicious acts. Additionally, human life expectancy has doubled in Western-style democracies over the last one hundred and fifty years; the wisdom of the elderly has an influence. The way we treat each other is improving. Morality is coming to be understood to be a complex mix of evolved tendencies, such as co-operation, compliance, fairness and reciprocity, plus attitudes developed by exposure to society in childhood, with an overlay of free choice. When Nietzsche desired morality to have a naturalistic source of value in the vital impulses of life itself, he didn't know how right he was.

What wicked of harmful acts could only a religious person perform thanks to their faith? Well looking only at Christianity alone we have seen all sorts of crimes against humanity: The Crusades, witch trials, The Spanish Inquisition, enslavement, homophobia etc, the list goes on and on when you examine history – but now ask yourself what valid and/or kind act could only a Christian perform which a secular individual could never do?

Christopher HITCHENS

SUMMARY OF CHAPTER 7

- Morality is not the exclusive property of Christians.
- The Bible is not a good moral compass.
- Behaving benignly under threat of 'eternal torture in hell' is not moral; it's immoral control by coercion.
- Behaving benignly for the promise of a reward in the form of 'eternal bliss in heaven' is not moral; it's immoral control by bribery.
- Killing in 'the Name of the Lord' is not moral; it's murder. Killers will not become 'martyrs' and will not get 72 virgins.
- Absolution from offensive behavior by swearing allegiance to a priestly representative of a non-evidential deity is not moral; it's a 'get out of jail free' card issued by a controller.
- Pillars of morality include empathy, reciprocity, nurturing, co-operation, compassion, consolation and fairness.
- Other social species exhibit moral behaviour to varying degrees; it is not exclusively human.
- Evidence indicates that moral behavior has evolved.
- It is an adaptation that benefits a population rather than specific individuals.
- We are born to behave co-operatively towards each other.
- Our infant brains develop in response to observed behaviour.
- Different human societies have different standards of morality – it matters where you are born!

- Morality is not absolute; it is mainly objective but sometimes expedient and always consequential.
- If you live a long life you can observe moral attitudes evolve!
- In extremis, we can act against our moral instincts to protect our family and friends or the vulnerable.
- Despite periods of behavior that are detrimental to human success, our 7.4 billion population is testament to our generally benign nature.
- The concepts of 'good' and 'evil' are attempts to polarise, into two fabricated categories, behaviors that are all actually facultative.

Richard Dawkins roundly refutes the myth that morality belongs to religion here: http://tinyurl.com/joto47c

The real killer question to ask theists on morals is, "If god told you to kill me, would you do it?" If they answer, "Yes", they are admitting to an intention to commit murder (a universal moral taboo), while if they answer, "No", they are revealing their morality is not god given!

We would all like to see humankind make progress towards a more benevolent and less malicious society, however, the way forward is *not* to cling to ancient unevidenced claims of absolute 'godly' moral certainty but to be open to modifying our attitudes in the light of circumstances, with an intention to improve relationships.

Theology has no salvageable theory of morality. Theists complain atheists have no reason to be moral. But in fact theists have no reason to actually be moral, as in: to elevate compassion, honesty, and reasonableness above all authority, even the authority of their own gods. Unless they covertly adopt a naturalistic moral theory (and most do), they are not actually moral people. They are minions. Theists are essentially the unquestioning gestapo of whatever monster manufactured the universe. Or rather, whatever monster some men made up and duped them into thinking it made the universe. Which means, they are essentially the gestapo of whatever random ignorant madmen wrote their scriptures and now thumps their pulpits with sufficiently fiery claims of special divine communications at bedtime.

Richard CARRIER

The greatest tragedy in mankind's entire history may be the hijacking of morality by religion

Arthur C CLARKE

7. WONDERLAND

Putting clothes on the ghost...

In November 2015, Andy Bannister posted a link to an event (http://tinyurl.com/jdrb863) that he hosted, and I started to watch his guest speaker, Dr. Nabeel Qureshi, whose opening remarks included this:

"I don't want to speak about whether God exists, I want to talk about what he is like" ! (my exclamation mark)

That's tantamount to me saying, "I don't want to speak about whether the Loch Ness Monster exists; I want to talk about what she is like!" Maybe she prefers kippers to courgettes and likes Brussels Sprouts with custard! Then he started to pray! At that point I gave up viewing the video; my life is too precious to waste it listening to people making unverifiable faith claims. I wouldn't give them a microphone!

How could anyone know what a god (or monster) is like, when there is not even evidence for its existence? Especially when there are so many self-appointed 'experts' in different faith systems each expressing their own ideas about what She is like, while simultaneously questioning everyone else's version of what She is like! This process enables Muslim scholars to assert that hundreds of eye-witnesses reported Mohammed's ascent to 'heaven' on a winged horse, but to deny that anyone saw Jesus rise from the dead. Meanwhile, Christian scholars will assure us that several witnesses *did* see Christ rise on the third day, but will reject claims that Mohammed flew to 'heaven' at all! Well, it doesn't take a genius to work out that they can't both be right but they can both be wrong!

Well, what *is* 'god' like? This is a bit like asking for detailed information about Humpty Dumpty! He was an egg so where was he laid? In a nest, or buried in the sand like a turtle's egg? What type of bird laid him or perhaps a reptile did – maybe it was a platypus? Did he need to be incubated? Was he going to hatch? Will the hatchling like to eat seeds or grubs? How did he come to get arms and legs and be dressed as a Victorian schoolboy? And was falling off the wall a compassionate act of suicide to absolve humanity from 'original sin'? Such unfathomable questions make me wonder... Are we are in *Wonderland?*

Over recent centuries, men have discovered many hitherto unknown beings and here's a rough description of how it often happens:

- A new creature is observed in its habitat, or signs of its existence are seen – e.g. skeletons, paw prints, dung
- A dead specimen is obtained
- It is dissected and its stomach contents are noted
- A live organism is caught
- Its behavior is studied in captivity
- More live specimens are captured
- They are bred in captivity and study continues

No one in their right mind makes much attempt to describe the detailed characteristics of a being *before we have even observed it...* That would be crazy speculation, wouldn't it?

The normal way of going about things is to investigate the claim of existence of an undiscovered being *prior* to assigning characteristics to it! Doing it in backwards order is no better than claiming that *it has terrible tusks and terrible claws and terrible teeth in its terrible jaws, knobbly knees and turned-out toes and a poisonous wart on the end of its nose!* That's fine for Julia Donaldson writing her excellent children's story, The Gruffalo, but it's not useful for adults trying to describe reality!

It's not possible to observe any of 'god's' characteristics because, we are told, She is invisible and 'immaterial'. Come to that, 'immaterial' itself is indistinguishable from imaginary! Ask yourself, is this a deliberate attempt to hoodwink us, or do believers not understand the meaning of 'hypothetical'? Maybe they are fooling *themselves*... What do *you* think?

So, since we have no evidence that *any* 'god' exists, we have a completely blank sheet of paper on which to write Her, entirely imaginary, characteristics! It's like the ultimate Desiderata[79]! Or a wish list for Santa Claus[80]!

Weirdly, the lack of evidence for a 'god' hasn't stopped a great many believers from putting clothes on this ghost. This ploy is the reverse of Hans Christian Anderson's great story, 'The Emperor's New Clothes'[81]. Instead of being about a naked Emperor and no clothes, there are wardrobes full of clothes but no evidence of an Emperor to wear them!

There have been many chapters to this saga; two of my favorite 'clothed gods' are Ixcacao[82], the Mayan goddess of chocolate and sex (it's hard to dislike her), and Cloacina[83] the goddess who allegedly kept Rome's sewers flowing - such a vital contribution! Thousands of 'gods', all but a few of them now discredited, have been profiled or have had whole biographies written about them. Unsurprisingly, most of the characteristics assigned to 'gods' are warm cuddly ones. Today, nobody wishes for a malicious and hateful 'god' like is reported in the Old Testament. That would be insane...

There are other non-evidential characters in our oral and written tradition: aliens, zombies, fairies, leprechauns and many more. Oddly, nobody has bothered to kit them out with quite the same level of detail, back story, etc. as the Christian 'god'. They seem only to have attracted serious attention since the beginning of the movie era. Is that because that's when it first became possible to make serious money out of charging punters for entertaining products? Spot a parallel anyone? Commercialization! Ask yourself, is the Disney Corporation the provider of fantasy for youngsters while churches cater for the wishful dreams of the older market?

How do Christians know that there is only *one* 'god' or that He is *their* favorite one? It's a reasonable question because the Jesus story shares a lot of features with the stories of other, earlier gods. Episodes like virgin birth, miracles and resurrection are show-stoppers that grab the attention of an incredulous audience. Take 'resurrection' for example: there's a list of 'resurrected gods' including Osiris, Horus, Isis, Tammuz, Adonis, Attis, Persephone, Dionysus and more. If you are looking for a 'once dead, now risen, god' you have plenty of choice! While Christ may be the single most popular 'god' *currently* (two billion identify as Christians allegedly[84]), that leaves about five billion people who are non-Christian. They are either giving credit (never *blame*, of course!) to other 'gods' or, sensibly, *not giving any credit to any 'god'*.

~~~

Andy's employer agrees with him (surprise!) and, in the Foreword to The Atheist Who Didn't Exist, he says,

"Time and again the atheist is unable to answer fundamental questions such as, 'Is there a moral framework to life?'"
Ravi ZACHARIA

Listen to me, Ravi, the reason some questions are called

'fundamental' is because *nobody* can answer them! They are *mysteries*. Why do you expect *'the atheist' (whoever that is)* to be able to answer such 'fundamental' questions? It's not as if 'atheists' have a research institute geared up for answering 'fundamental' questions! You might as well complain that a motley assemblage of butchers, bakers and candlestick-makers can't answer such questions!

One thing you may have noticed is that, *unlike theists*, 'the atheist' *doesn't claim to be able* to answer these 'fundamental questions'. Is this because 'atheists', in the 'ideological policy-making organization' sense that Christians like to misrepresent them, don't actually exist? Could it be that Andy's book title needs a bit of editing? Should, 'The Atheist Who Didn't Exist' be called simply, 'Atheists Don't Exist'?

207

Ravi, it's you theists who make claims of having answers, which you do without the backing of any evidence! Dear reader, which would you rather be, an honest non-believer who admits they don't know, for no reward, or a theist who deceives, *and gets financial remuneration,* by pretending to have answers that they actually *don't have?* Isn't such deception a crime? (See UK Fraud Act 2006[85])

Scientific investigation is self-evidently the best method for discovering answers, but it has neither finished the job, nor is it co-terminous with 'atheism'. In fact, the vast majority of 'atheists' are *not* scientists. And an inability to answer 'fundamental' questions is not a license for *inventing* 'answers'! We have priests for doing that! They have a hotline to 'god', the 'creator deity', allegedly!

Over the millennia, two main types of 'god' have been dreamed up to 'answer' our questions: 'gods' of Nature and Manlike 'gods'. Most of the early 'gods' were 'spirits' occupying natural things, like rivers, rain, thunder, the sun and volcanoes. Early man had no understanding not only of *how* the world worked, but also no inkling of how to *discover* how things worked. So inventing a 'godly explanation' was more comforting than the fearful insecurity of ignorance. Having a 'god' meant people could worship, perform sacrifices and pray for better weather, for more milk from their goats or protection from illness. This allowed them to *feel* that they were *doing something* to get them out of their predicaments or, at least, to distract them from their wretched circumstances.

Religion is like homeopathy for the mind. Snake-oil salesmen soon realized they could earn off local beliefs by 'confirming' the 'gods' with a theatrical ritual in return for donations, and so religion was born! It's such a good business! There are no costly raw materials to purchase, no guarantees to finance, every member freely promotes the company by inducting their children and we pay the leaders for the privilege! In the UK people have been compensated for the payment protection insurance scam foisted on them by the banks in the 1990s, what about us getting back our tithes and offerings from churches whose promises have not been fulfilled?

The early pantheon, called 'Animism', was polytheistic with a bewildering array of nature-spirit deities. Having so many 'gods' made it difficult for would-be despots, claiming to be a god's representative, to consolidate power over an entire population into their hands in the way that they desired. That's why manlike 'gods', which evolved from intermediate species of half man/half animal 'gods' such as Anubis, Osiris and Sobek[86], have largely superseded natural 'spirit' deities.

Making 'gods' in the image of man meant that priests could

imbue them with human emotions like jealousy and wrath. This enabled the creation of artworks and stories featuring heroic characters that people could easily identify with, thus capturing an audience's imagination. Then clergy could bring about mass crowd control. Donations started to come in not only from followers, but also from rulers who, perceiving their influence over the population, sponsored them to keep them onboard. It's a win:win strategy that still works today[87]!

Gradually the god concepts were whittled down from many specialist gods, every one a supposed 'force' in their own particular field such as the weather, crops or hunt and each with their own 'prophets', to a few multitasking gods, and finally to *one all-purpose 'god'*. Monotheism had arrived. Concentrating the attributes of many 'gods' into a *single 'all-powerful being'* shrewdly focused 'authority' onto a few Earthly 'representatives', like the Pope, who could control society by promising 'salvation', selling 'forgiveness', conducting ceremonies and, *most importantly,* could be the ultimate recipients of all contributions; the 'Mr Big' of the outfit.

When all 'explanations' are attributed to *your* 'god', the one you claim to have a 'personal relationship with', you have more 'services' to sell and will get rich quicker than the priest who can only sell one trick, like claiming to be able to make it rain. Monotheism is a better business model than polytheism.

210

Let's face it; husbands and wives, sons and fathers, daughters and mothers in the same family often disagree about what 'god' is like and what 'She wants'. However, top of the list of desired attributes for a 'god' is *power*. From earliest times, 'gods' have been expected to be able to perform feats well beyond human capabilities. What would be the point of a 'god' who couldn't do the things that we wish to get done but can't do for ourselves? They *have* to be Super-beings; nobody wishes for a feeble 'god'; that would be *embarrassing!*

THERE, THERE, YOU POOR, PUNY LITTLE GOD.
I WON'T LET THEM BULLY YOU...

Sebastian

211

Some of the 'clothes' that 'god' has been dressed in are nonsensical: contradictory 'powers' like omnipotence, omniscience, omnipresence and *omnibenevolence* (which seems to have gained traction more recently than the others). Why do I say they are contradictory?

Well, take omnipotence for a start, an omnipotent 'god' would presumably be able to create a mass so large She wouldn't be able to lift it; but, surely, that same omnipotent 'god' should be able to lift *any* weight? So omnipotence is *internally* contradictory. (Christians have a contorted defense for this)

Now take omniscience, this is taken to mean that 'god' knows everything that has happened and everything that will happen. Knowing what will happen fits in with the idea of 'god' having a plan and, therefore, it denies mankind freewill and invalidates prayer. It also means that She would be unable to make changes because that would reveal Her foreknowledge to have been incorrect, unless She knew in advance that She was going to change her plan an unspecified number of times, which is a wager, not foreknowledge at all! So 'god' can either have omniscience with an unchangeable plan that denies us freewill and makes prayer a waste of time, in which case She cannot be omnipotent, *or* She can have the power of change (omnipotence), permit us to have freewill and respond to our prayers, in which case She is not omniscient!

And omnipresence could only be true if 'god' exists in 'hell' as well as everywhere else. Is that likely? As for omnibenevolence, just watch the daily news of natural disasters and form an opinion about the benevolence towards humanity of this supposedly 'all powerful loving god'...

'GODLY POWERS'

Omniscience	Omnipotence	Omnipresence	Omnibenevolence
Has Foreknowledge	Has Power to Change	Is Everywhere	Universally good
Has an Unchangeable Plan, Humans can't have free-will	'God' has no Foreknowledge and no plan but humans *can* have free-will	Must be in 'Hell' with 'Satan'!	Prevents disaster or rescues from harm
Can't respond to Prayer	Could respond to Prayer		
Can't be Omnipotent	Can't be Omniscient	Reconcile that!	Not according to the news!

213

Debating with theists can be rather frustrating. Since they have no evidence for their belief system, they are reduced to challenging the worldview of their 'opponent', which, as they see it, is the scientific position. They criticize science for not having answers to 'fundamental' questions, conveniently overlooking the mountain of phenomena that scientists *do have* explanations for. They point out that scientists only have hypotheses at the frontiers of science and then claim that we are no better than them with their godunnit explanation. These are examples of the Tu Quoque fallacy – attacking our honestly admitted ignorance (and ongoing investigations) on grounds that can also be applied to their *own* claims, which they are *not* willing to admit are much weaker. That's acting like a 'home referee': showing a bias for their own side!

Isn't it hypocritical to criticize us instead of defending their own hypothesis? Especially when there is a huge inequity of evidence between the two positions? Scientists are building a portfolio, theists are defending an empty cupboard and have no method of filling it, no strategy for discovery. We would all like to have all our questions instantly answered, but scientific investigation is a work in progress and the job is not finished yet. If it *were* all done, scientific investigation would stop! One thing is for certain; the answers are not in an Iron Age book! Ask yourself, are we likely to find solutions that we don't know today in a book written back when we hardly knew *anything?*

Theists point out that scientific answers are mostly based on induction and therefore are never certain; this is another Tu Quoque Fallacy since their belief system is also vulnerable to that accusation. Well, it's true inductive logic is only probabilistic and is based on the latest state of evidence, but surely *some* evidence is better than none! For all its lack of absolute certainty, science does an amazingly good job of describing nature. Furthermore, scientists are honest about the provisional status of their information, unlike priests who claim to have *certain* knowledge *without any evidence!*

But pointing out the weaknesses in a rival position is not supporting one's own proposition. We call that an *Argument from Ignorance Fallacy* – basing a conclusion on what is *not known* rather than providing positive evidence to back your own hypothesis. Colloquially it's called the 'God of the Gaps' argument, and the gaps in which the 'godunnit' explanation can still be proposed have been shrinking. We no longer have need of the 'Rain God', for example.

215

Over the centuries, thinking men have questioned theists about the *whereabouts* of the 'god' they claim exists. The conversation has gone like this (I'm using Andy's tactic of writing both sides of a conversation to suit my agenda here!):

Person A: *"Is 'god' on Earth?"*
Person B: *"No, He's in the clouds."*
Person A: *"So, 'god' is in the atmosphere?"*
Person B: *"No, He's in the heavens."*
Person A: *"Ah, 'god' is in the Universe then?"*
Person B: *"No, He's immaterial and outside of the Universe."*

That's the 'Moving the Goalposts' fallacy. Every time we demonstrate the lack of evidence for 'god' in some recently understood realm, He moves to a new imaginary location!

"I know! He's inside your head! That's where She is!"

Considering that ALL the answers we have discovered so far have shown that questions have *natural* explanations, the 'godunnit' option is getting *increasingly* improbable and unreasonable as days go by...

Another theistic trick to watch out for is the Ad Hoc Hypothesis Fallacy. This is where a believer tries to defend their 'god' hypothesis by fabricating another hypothesis in an effort to render the first one unfalsifiable. An example would

216

be the attempt to cover up for our failure to observe 'god' over the last two thousand years, by claiming that *She is 'immaterial' and therefore unobservable.* The period throughout which She has *not been observed* coincides with an enormous *increase in our ability to observe*, thanks to the development of many instruments that can detect phenomena previously invisible to human senses, and yet we *still* haven't found Her.

The fact is, 'immateriality' is *another* hypothetical concept, just a mental construct in the Conceptual Realm, not *evidence* for a hypothetical 'god'. We need to find out whether this mental construct matches reality. The only way this can be done is by scientific investigation. Scientific investigation is like saying to the universe, *"I have this philosophical idea, is it correct?"*

I recommend asking theists what is the difference between 'immaterial' and 'unreal' or between the Supernatural Realm and Fantasyland. If they can't answer that satisfactorily, they are effectively saying that the reason we have no observations of a creator deity may be because She *isn't real!*

Theists tend to draw a line between materialism (reality) and immaterialism - the undetectable refuge where they hide their deity to protect it from being falsified. The line should actually be drawn between the Natural Realm and the Conceptual

217

Realm. The Conceptual Realm is where our thoughts are conceived – in the incredibly sophisticated software of the brain. Having these fantastic brains means there are no limits to what we can conceive (imagine). This is well illustrated by the impossible art of M C Escher and others. Our inventive minds, the algorithms running on our neurons, can create all sorts of propositions and the only way we can discover whether they are feasible or not is by testing against reality to find out if they match observations. The jet engine design concept *did* stand up to such scrutiny. Phlogiston *didn't* and Humpty Dumpty didn't even start out with an intention of reflecting reality (but he is still conceivable – as an egg dressed in a Victorian schoolboy uniform!).

Some will try to defend the 'immaterial' proposition by pointing to mathematics and logic and saying triumphantly, "See, *those things* are immaterial. There *is* such a thing as immateriality!" That is a category error. Math and logic are *conceptual*, not 'immaterial'. The connection is the *other way round*: 'immateriality' is merely a concept rather than those concepts being 'immaterial'. There is no evidence for anything 'immaterial', and if something immaterial were to be discovered, it would promptly have to be redesignated as material.

So, math and logic are *concepts*, mental constructs that can be used to model reality closely and are useful tools (as is language) but, unfortunately, 'immateriality' has not been verified or even validated. It remains a hypothetical claim, as does 'god' Herself. Ask yourself; can we substantiate a claim with *another claim?*

The next theistic ploy is to refer to quantum non-locality and entanglement and gloat, *"You can't explain that, can you!"* Well, no, we can't. At least not yet, but *our ignorance is not evidence for your 'god' either.* Once we discovered the physics behind thunder and lightning those phenomena were no longer attributed to the gods – Thor was put out of a job!

But had we not managed to discover their causes would 'Godunnit' *really explain* them? No. In fact not one phenomenological mystery in the history of our species has ever turned out to have a godly explanation and yet thousands upon thousands of former mysteries have clearly been shown to have natural explanations.

And please don't think that non-believers lack the capacity for wonder. Perhaps we find the vastness of the universe and the diversity of life even *more* wonderful because *understanding a phenomenon does not diminish the wonder, it accentuates it.*

SUMMARY OF CHAPTER 7

- It's foolish to assign characteristics to a being that may not exist.
- Find it first then *investigate* it to discover what its properties actually are!
- Questions are not answers – scientific ignorance is not proof that a 'god' did anything.
- Scientists can wonder with the best of us!

If your God is powerful, why would it need anything from you?
Lance SIEVERT

The church doesn't like the people to grow up because you can't control grown-ups, that's why we talk about being 'born again'. If you're 'born again' you're still a child.
Bishop John Shelby SPONG

8. WORDS, DAMN WORDS

In The Atheist That Doesn't Exist, Andy writes several passages using the word 'supernatural' and he deduces that:

"Atheists don't need god, or deities, or heaven, or an afterlife, or the supernatural,"

The fact that Andy can write a clause with subtended phrases like that shows how different our minds are! He obviously doesn't know it, but that partial sentence is powerfully polarizing. Theists will look at it and think, *"Those arrogant atheists! How dare they dismiss God and everything to do with Him?"* While non-believers will read the same words and wonder if it's a tongue-in-cheek send up of the religious mindset. Andy doesn't seem to realize that six of the fourteen words in his sentence are *just conceptual items*. Theists are often so uncritically brought up in 'The Language of The Lord' that they regard the words 'atheists', 'god', 'deities', 'heaven', 'afterlife' and 'supernatural' as being *actual real things!* Ask yourself, what if they are all make believe, merely *imaginary notions?* Let's substitute the ideas of 'Fairyland' for those theistic words and then you'll understand how it sounds to me:

"Afairyists don't need Tinker Bell, or fairies, or fairyland, or an afterfairylife, or the superfairydom,"

221

You see? *Once we exchange all the words that are meaningless to non-believers with words that are meaningless to **everyone**,* there is nothing left! No wonder 'atheists' *don't need any of it!* Why would non-believers, or anyone else for that matter, **need** *ideas that have no evidence of existence?* Air, water, food and shelter are what we need. Yes, we may *want* a fast car and, in the same way, theists seem to want a 'god' and all the 'godly' accoutrements that come with it. This language issue requires another entire book to address properly; one that I may write if I live long enough!

Way back in the past, English was peppered with pagan notions (like 'Green Man', a rural mythological being, but now just a pub name) that eventually lost their cultish significance and, maybe one day in the future, everyone will learn a neutral non-religious vocabulary, but Christian propaganda is currently so embedded in our language that I don't see that happening any time soon! In the meanwhile, let's take a look at three key Christian words: faith, sin and evil.

FAITH

'Faith' is one of the most contentious words. Bertrand Russell once said,

"Where there is evidence, no-one speaks of faith. We do not speak of faith that two and two are four or that the Earth is round. We only speak of faith when we wish to substitute

222

emotion for evidence."

After centuries of propagandizing, theists have turned 'faith' around to mean the very opposite of what it should mean. Here are some of Andy's thoughts on faith:

You see, here's the thing: everybody has faith; everybody is religious. Being religious is simply part of what being a human being is. I think that some atheists find this idea frightening, because it means there is hard thinking to be done. You can't simply say, "Prove your religion to me", then cross your arms like a traffic warden with a bad case of hemorrhoids. Everybody has beliefs that are central for them, beliefs that cause actions, beliefs that define them, beliefs that have implications. And for those kinds of beliefs we can be asked to give reasons.

Naturally, theists want to make out that everybody has faith – they don't want to be thought of as *odd!* Andy may be right about there being a human tendency towards a religious style of beliefs (see my first book on this subject, Godbuster, available from Amazon and on tablet), but please notice that he starts out talking about 'faith' and ends up talking about 'belief'. He makes no distinction. To him, faith just seems to be belief on steroids! *And* he seems to patronizingly believe that he knows the minds of 'atheists' better than 'they' do 'themselves'! Insultingly, Andy implies that 'atheists' are *frightened of hard thinking*; he can't resist a sneaky bit of ad

223

hominem! Yet it's 'atheists' who are supposed to be the aggressive or 'militant' ones...

Later, Andy uses 'faith' in a different way. In Chapter 10 of The Atheist Who Didn't Exist he writes two more of his parables: *The Panini Poisoner of Pimlico* and the story of *Secularist Sidney who attended the Reason Rally*. They are fun to read so I recommend them, (Andy's book is full of great fiction but devoid of facts!) although I don't have the space to reproduce them here. In that chapter he claims we all must have faith in all sorts of things every day. See here:

Whether it's life's more philosophical questions - the reality of our conscious experience, why science works, the existence of other minds - or whether it's just the mundane realities of life - flying on a plane, undergoing a medical procedure, sipping a latte, using my credit card - every day I exercise faith in numerous little ways.

Here Andy is mixing up 'faith' with belief, trust and confidence. Oh, how scientists dislike words that have imprecise meanings! Communication fails if we have no agreement between us about the meanings of the words we are using. Faith should not be considered to be synonymous with confidence or trust. We need distinct definitions for all of these words. Sadly, ordinary dictionaries are not much help. Take 'precise' and 'accurate' for example. Dictionaries usually tell us they are synonyms. This is incorrect: 'precision' is about how *near* you get to a target, while 'accuracy' is about how *often* you hit it.

But first of all, let's deal with his question *'why science works'*. The statement *'science works'* is not a matter of faith. It's not even a matter for belief. Look around you – the fact that science works is very evidential. Are you reading this on a tablet – see what I mean? All the artefacts of modern civilization are plentiful indication of science's effective working. Remember Chapter 3? It showed how *evidential information* does not need actively believing. 'Science works' is what Andy called a THING THAT IS. It's not a proposition that is in question. Our computers are evidence for that. Don't waste your time believing it, save your belief for *dubious* propositions, for hypotheses such as, 'there is a creator deity'.

As for *'why'* science works: it's because *we've deliberately invented it to do that!* We've steadily improved our methods of investigation until they enable the production of effective models of the Natural Realm. That's its purpose. That's *why*. We can do that. We can supply purpose: organisms are purposeful, inorganic matter and processes are not. Seeking a purposeful explanation for inanimate natural events like the origin of the universe, or claiming that it must mean Godunnit is a Category Error.

Now let us take a look at 'confidence' by adopting Andy's example of *'using my credit card'*. We all accept that money has value and the way we observe other people using currency is consistent with this. I can go out and repeatedly gather evidence demonstrating that money is considered to be a tradable commodity. Once we accept that evidence enables us to *conclude* something, we no longer have to give that something our belief. Facts based on evidence do not require actively believing. We don't daily doubt our cash anymore than we doubt gravity. Evidence makes the need for active belief evaporate; we don't have to constantly reiterate our belief in notes and coins. The Chancellor doesn't talk about belief or faith in the currency; he talks about *confidence* in it. Confidence in legal tender is shown *quantifiably* in the exchange rate. Of course, just as in science, *new* observations can shake this confidence – a bank collapse for example, and then the previously unquestioned information may have to be re-examined. In the meantime, however, it's safe to suspend active belief in the fact that our currency has value because it's a probable truth.

Confidence is a *measurable* quantity, a *numerical* concept. It's a statistical probability. We can have high confidence in another of Andy's examples - the safety of *'flying on a plane'* because only one person dies for every two billion person-miles flown. Whereas we should have low confidence in the safety of motorcycles because two hundred and fifty people are killed for every two billion person-miles traveled. Take Andy's next example, *'undergoing a medical procedure'*. I was told before my heart surgery that only 2-3% of patients died as a result of the operation, consequently I had enough confidence to give my consent (and I am much improved as a result, thanks for asking). Confidence is based on empirical data. Faith is not the same as confidence.

Now let's look at trust. Trust is also based on reputation but it may not be so easily measured. For example, we might trust an airport's security systems if the airport has never had an incident – that's a good track record, but there isn't a complete data set to base our opinion on because the security of the airport may never have been seriously challenged, so we have no numbers. We can have a QUALITATIVE trust for it rather than QUANTITATIVE confidence, but trust is not faith either.

Ancient religious texts (or modern ones for that matter) are worse than that airport: they are *hearsay* not evidence, that's why you have to give them your faith. If you think they are reliable, ask yourself whether you can believe on faith alone that Mohammed flew up to paradise on the back of a winged horse. You can't? Now ask any Muslim whether he has faith that Christ was born of a virgin or rose from the dead and you'll find that he thinks that requires the 'wrong sort of faith' – as if there actually could be a 'right' kind! This is because faith is really about pretending to know something that you simply *cannot* know. No one can. Unlike confidence and trust, *faith* is what you have to resort to when you have *neither* QUANTIFIABLE measures of reliability (confidence) *nor* QUALITATIVE reputation (trust) to go on.

As Bertrand Russell indicated, evidence-based information negates any need for faith. Personally, I would go a little further and say that evidence even removes the need for active believing. Evidence turns propositions into THINGS THAT ARE. Do astronomers need to congregate in special halls and stand in line chanting? Ask yourself, why not?

Scientists don't need any faith; they can simply observe planetoid Pluto's trajectory around the sun and calculate that its 'year' takes 248 Earth years to complete one orbit, even though we have only known about its existence since 1942. Despite the fact that no one has ever seen a *whole* circuit happen, an extremely robust mathematical formula accurately describes where Pluto was yesterday, last week, last month and last year and testable predictions can be made for where it should be tomorrow. This is very strong independently observable evidence that the formula is a good model and highly likely to be accurate in the future. *'Model'* is the important word.

On the other hand, religious faith has an appalling track record! For example, intercessory prayer is no more successful at speeding up the recovery of patients from a heart condition than results by chance, and this fact isn't some 'one off' statistic. The Richard Dawkins Foundation reports that this is actually the conclusion of his nemesis, The Templeton Foundation[88], which throws huge sums of money at attempts to give some degree of scientific credibility to faith claims. It's great that theists want scientific verification but good scientists shouldn't set out intending to *'prove'* their hypothesis anyway – that's not open minded.

The Templeton Foundation's multimillion-dollar research program backfired badly when its results were examined because it actually showed that if a patient *knew* they were being prayed for, they took *longer* to recover statistically speaking, whereas the patients who *didn't know* they were being prayed for recovered at the same *faster* rate as the patients who were *not* being prayed for at all! A negative correlation was the last thing Templeton wanted or expected! The only rational inference that can be drawn from these statistics is that the people who knew they were being prayed for actually felt that they had some sort of obligation to 'perform' better, which made them feel more stressed and the stress proved to be detrimental to their recovery. Therefore, the logical thing to do if a friend or relative of yours is seriously ill in hospital is to *make sure you don't tell them that you'll pray for them!*

You can pray if you want to, (please understand that a multi-million-dollar study has statistically demonstrated that secretly praying for them has no demonstrable effect on their health what-so-ever) but *telling* them that you're praying for them will actually *damage* their recovery! Overt prayer is harmful! If you want the evidence (you should demand it) take a look at this link: http://tinyurl.com/j7xcujk

Andy says the clue to understanding 'faith' is in its origin from 'fides' meaning 'trust' and 'reliability' (why doesn't he accept the etymological meaning of 'Atheist' then?) and he asks:

When we trust somebody are we simply being naïve, or even discriminatory? Should I just flip a coin at breakfast each morning to decide whom I'll trust most that day - Honest Joe the Genuine Low mileage Used-Honda Salesman, or my wife, to whom I've been happily married for sixteen years?
(Abridged for brevity)

Andy goes on to reveal that it's his wife who has developed the track record of reliability necessary to lead him to trust her (that's good for him!), but he equates this *trust based on reputation* with *faith* in her likely behavior. That's not what faith is. Trust is based on good reputation, faith is applied *despite* there being *no* good reputation. Faith is *misplaced* trust in the *absence* of evidence or reputation. Trusting Honest Joe the car salesman is what would require faith.

However, both Honest Joe and Andy's wife are members of a highly evolved species: Homo sapiens. So there's reason to think that they might have inherited genetic traits that have made them both trustworthy to *some* extent. It's certainly possible that either or both may not be *100% trustworthy*, but at least Andy has *some* evidence they could be: more in his wife perhaps, and less in Joe, but none-the-less *something*. Ask yourself, how much evidence does Andy have that the Christian 'god' is trustworthy? Precisely none!

Andy has no evidence that his 'God' of the Bible is any more reliable than the Pagan 'gods'. Yet not so long ago, those Pagan 'gods' were very popular. If current birthrate trends continue as they have been going for quite some time now, *Allah* is next in line to be top 'god'. Ask yourself, when Zeus and Thor were fashionable were they somehow more evidential than any invisible deity then or now? Nope. When it comes to support, *something*, no matter how minuscule, is always better than *nothing* and empty claims in ancient books (or modern ones for that matter) amount to nothing where extraordinary powers are concerned! (Unless you really think that Harry Potter can ride on a broomstick...)

Blurring our language to support their presuppositions is an art that many theists have mastered. Peter Boghossian, author of *A Manual for Creating Atheists*, (buy it – it's good!) is a kindred spirit of mine who recognizes a particular problem with the word 'faith' and he does a presentation on how we should redefine it. See it here: http://tinyurl.com/z9qmren

EVIL AND SIN

Another couple of misleading words in the Christian lexicon are 'evil' and 'sin'. Theists tend to use them to characterize transgressions against *their* version of morality (not against the moral codes of any rival faith, of course; it's another example of the divisiveness of religions).

Andy says:

If 'atheism' is true, calling anything 'evil' is problematic, as all we really have are assorted personal preferences, just a bag of assorted pick-and-mix from the moral candy store.

Earlier in his book Andy asserted that 'atheism' is an ideology or belief system (remember when he described it as a *fundamentalism?*). Now he is claiming that it is merely *personal preferences!* In truth, there *is* no 'atheism' of either sort (so it can't be 'true' – that's just nonsense). There is no *ideology* of 'atheism' and *personal preferences* do not constitute 'atheism', unless choosing not to put sugar in coffee makes you into an 'asugarist'! I wish he'd make up his mind about which Straw Man he is attacking! Is he deliberately changing his description of 'atheism' just to liven up his propaganda? Is that allowed?

"Which misrepresentation of atheism shall I use today?"

Of course, we have a much greater basis for morality than mere personal preferences. Personal preferences are what we use to decide whether to buy a latte or a cappuccino. Morals come *not* from the bible, which is a very poor example of how to behave, but from much deeper, more foundational roots. We can observe moral behavior in other species; it has evolved in order to facilitate the success of a population. For example, murder is obviously detrimental to that outcome in principle, but may be expedient on occasions. (see Chap. 7)

However, Andy is right: calling anything 'evil' *is* problematic, but not just for 'atheists', and not for the reason he imagines. It's because 'evil' is a purely theistic word that has no relevance to society or science. It assumes that there is an *absolute* standard of morality to obey, *and* that only the Christian god can dispense it. That's simply incorrect; morality is often contingent. Sociologists do not even use the word 'evil'. What's it supposed to mean? *A sucking vortex of antisocial behavior as defined by Christians and only by Christians?*

THE PLUGHOLE OF EVIL!

Sebastian

The Bible disapproves of mixed fiber garments, eating shellfish and is proscriptive about sex! It's the same with the fictional concepts of 'Satan' and 'Hell'. *And* it's yet another example of how *a single sentence* by Andy takes several paragraphs for me to unpack...

235

And 'sin', what's that? *'An umbrella of naughtiness'?*

Yes, we can be influenced by antisocial behavior in others, especially when young, because our personal adaptive tendencies are still 'crystallizing' as our brain lays down more neurons and builds more connections, so we are even more ready to comply with leadership examples. That's why parents disapprove of unadmirable role models or 'bad influences'.

So, how do we decide what is detrimental? In a number of

ways – a behavior might be unfair (many social animals understand fair sharing), it might be malicious (empathy enables us to identify hurtful actions), it might be unhelpful to the wellbeing of a vulnerable person such as refusal to groom another, etc. Actions that we agree communally are undesirably harmful to the betterment of society are not *sins*; they are either rude, uncaring antisocial actions or they have been designated *crimes*. Obviously, this does not include infringements that have not been democratically agreed – *they* are obviously bogus offences imposed for the benefit of a tyrannical leadership and no one else; heresy, blasphemy and apostasy come into this category. I would contend that cruel and unusual punishments are also not conducive to species success because they are psychologically damaging to all those involved, even to the perpetrators. Post Traumatic Stress Disorder does not help pair bonding, reproduction and nurturing: the pathways to Biological accomplishment.

The Christian way of thinking has resulted from the need perceived by early religious leaders to secure their income by personifying the 'one true god' story in order to capture maximum public attention. We love to identify with characters in a tale and we will pay for that entertainment. Claiming ownership of access to a moral authority has given clergy the power to sell permissions or 'forgiveness' for a price and, as a result of living in this bubble of a jurisdiction, church leaders can act dictatorially towards their staff even in a democratic country by claiming that their allegiance is to a 'higher authority' than national or international law – to 'god'.

~~~

There was no concept of 'sin' or 'evil' in pantheism; in fact many 'gods' were themselves tyrannical and 'immoral', a theme that was carried over into the Old Testament where the consolidation of 'godly powers' into the single deity of monotheism enabled a more gripping narrative because 'He' could be given what dramatists might call a 'three dimensional' character. This involved 'Him' giving approval or disapproval to behaviors in a familiarly parental manner. Sadly for believers, evidence for the existence of such an entity is entirely lacking.

Let's face it; divisions are not helpful to the maintenance of a peaceful human society. Some divisions are real and unavoidable and the best we can do is trivialize them and learn to tolerate them. This is the way to accommodate differences like skin color[77] and location of birth. Other differences, such as speech and culture, we can work on to improve our ability to communicate and understand each other, while disparities such as wealth need to be equalized. What we could well do without though, are *false* divisions, such as ones based on hypothetical 'gods', which have

238

human agents who recruit our language to serve them with their own lexicon and divide humanity into *us* and *them*: *my 'true God's' people* and *your 'false god's' people* or *'you godless folk'* – the gentiles, heathens, infidels and atheists.

~~~

Our conceptual ability is boundless so we can conceive of anything, even stories to bolster religious beliefs like Andy's modern-day parables. Scientists separate correct concepts from false ones by 'asking the universe' for feedback on them. Theists should be taking a leaf from the scientists' book and asking, "Does my hypothesis match observations and would anyone be able to demonstrate that I am wrong if I *was* mistaken?" They need more doxastic openness — willingness to revise their beliefs when presented with contrary evidence.

Theists don't do the investigation stage; instead they allow themselves to get sidelined by gathering evidence for *the scenery*, such as a cave with a stone door, rather than for *the action*. If the reality of a location is evidence for the events in a story, then Harry Potter must be true because some of it is set at 'Platform 9 3/4 in King's Cross, which is a genuine London railway station!

But obtaining evidence for two thousand year old events is

impossible without a time machine. Furthermore, the claimed 'miracles' are not feasible, according to science! Events are dynamic; once they've happened they are over and can no longer be observed. Oddly, theists complain that the fossil record is not evidence of events of change happening but they don't apply that criticism to their own claims of historic events! (The fossil record is not evidence of change itself, but a dated sequence of a progression of organisms coming into and going out of existence is consistent with the idea that change has occurred, whereas there is nothing significant that is consistent with resurrection or virgin birth.)

Yes, we can *conceive* of a 'god' but, so far, when we have asked the universe for feedback in the form of evidence for our 'god' concept, answer comes there none. Scientists demand evidence and accept that we have to put up with a provisional model that is as close a match to observations as possible. On the other hand, theists have no evidence for their claims yet they assert them with dogmatic certainty.

Logic doesn't conclude anything; it just helps us to decide which are our better ideas, the ones that are worth testing, and which ones to dump. Unfortunately, we commonly take 'proof' to be stronger than evidence. It's the other way round. Evidence is real; proof is merely conceptual. We still have to 'ask the universe' (check by investigating for observations) whether this or that proven logical concept matches with reality. Ask yourself, does it make sense to build an entire belief system on an *unevidenced hypothesis of a creator deity*? To do so is exactly like all Ufologists deciding that flying saucers are like the craft described in Howard Hugh's 'Earth versus The Flying Saucers' and *not* like the craft seen in Steven Spielberg's 'Close Encounters Of The Third Kind'. Why assume *either* is correct when we have no empirical evidence for *any* alien spacecraft visiting Earth? (It's highly improbable that aliens have visited because of the time required to travel the vast distances even at light speed, which is probably fatal to a physical body.)

Theists of all complexions have constructed whole panoplies of properties on their particular 'god' hypotheses. None of them have been evidential. They are all merely conceptual: just inside their heads with no match to observations. Yet they dogmatically assert their veracity and demonize opponents to the point of deadly conflict. If there *were* such a thing as 'evil', religion would be a close match to it. Most faiths express the opinion that only *they* possess the 'truth', so all the others are seen as simply wrong. This dogmatic polarizing is hardly a useful way of conducting peaceful relations in a world containing wildly differing values and outlooks. In fact it's a recipe for disaster, whereas an evidence-driven outlook is *not* harmful because it's beyond dispute.

241

In the absence of evidence, people fall back on beliefs, on opinions. Opinions and beliefs *can* be chosen by an individual himself or herself but, usually, an influential adult instills them in childhood. 'Getting them young' is the reason behind religious naming ceremonies like Baptisms and genital labeling like circumcision.

Another thing we are fond of doing is making 'by definition' one of the premises or parts of an argument. Forgive me but aren't definitions just human fabricated concepts? I define a pint of beer on the table before me! Nope, that didn't work!

We need to look out for where the conceptual leap is in philosophical reasoning. It might be in the uncertainty of a premise, the fabrication of a definition or the non-derivability of the 'conclusion'. What about the data? We can't always be sure we have a complete data set: Ptolemy thought he had all he needed to know about the behavior of the sun when he came up with his geocentric model of the 'spheres of the heavens'. Then the telescope was invented... Even if there is no apparent flaw in the logic yet, an argument remains just a conceptualization until it is supported or refuted by evidence. Until then it's just a proposed mental model, an association of ideas, nothing more.

Syllogizing premises into a deduction in a brain means no more than a person/persons has/have perceived a correlation. As we know from statistics, a correlation has no significance on its own. Until an actual *correspondence to reality* has been observed, it's just a notion in the Conceptual Realm. One check that can be performed is to construct a reverse argument and ask how reasonable it is. Philosopher Stephen Law exemplifies this technique in his 'evil god' refutation of theism see here http://tinyurl.com/ht9wgrl

Where Believers and Scientists differ is in their attitude towards logic. Scientists recognize that logic is a useful tool for constructing hypotheses or designing investigations but they realize that thought, which is all logic is, is subordinate to evidence. Even after evidence has been gathered, Scientists are trained to keep an open mind to the possibility of *new* evidence arriving that challenges the current understanding, *whereas believers dogmatically assert their certainty of their non-evidential doctrines that are only supported by thought and argument.*

Before I leave this subject, here is a warning: if you're in the company of meteorologists, don't call the weather 'unpredictable'. You would be impugning their ability to forecast! Use the word 'changeable'. When speaking with scientists, employ language with great care and precision.

243

HOW TO TELL ARGUMENT FROM EVIDENCE

ARGUMENT	EVIDENCE
Internally fabricated within a brain or brains Conceptual	Externally available in the Natural Realm to anyone. Observed not conceptual
Premises may be false	Repetition removes doubt
Involves an interpretive step - Identifying a correlation	Observations either match prediction or don't match it
The quality depends on the ability of the arguer	Quality is independent of the ability of the observer
Remains hypothetical until confirmed or denied by observations	Is the inspector that distinguishes good arguments from bad
Delivers deductions, inductions and abductions	Delivers conclusions – evidential information
Disputable	Currently Indisputable*

* If it's disputable, it's not evidence; it's opinion.

Example: If several people, on several different occasions, observe a bird visiting my garden, we have repeated independent evidence of bird-visits. We can have opinions about what that means – for example: Is it the same bird? Is it several identical birds each making a few visits? Where are they coming from? Where are they going to? But we can't dispute the repeated independent observations: my garden has had multiple bird-visits: fact.

Observations are one thing, conclusions are another...

ENGLISH TO CHRISTISH DICTIONARY

	ENGLISH	CHRISTISH
ACT OF GOD	Disaster	Salvation
ADULTERY	Consensual sex between adults	Sin punishable by stoning
AFTERLIFE	Death	Eternal existence
AGNOSTIC	'God' doubter	Wimpish atheist
ANGEL	Really cute little girl	A pretty winged woman by God's side
APOSTASY	Leaving a religion	Quitting the faith and going to Hell
ASCENSION	Rising	Move up to heaven
ATHEIST	Disbeliever in 'god'	Immoral, purposeless God-hater to pray for
BAPTISM	Baby naming ceremony	Induction into parents' church to ensure its continued business
BASTARD	Mean person	Fatherless child
BELIEF	Personally chosen attitude towards a proposition	True fact, because the Bible says so (except for the nasty bits – they are being taken out of context)
BIBLE	Ancient religious text like Qur'an	God's words – all true (unlike the Qur'an)
BLASPHEMY	Bogus crime	Punishable insult to God or Jesus
CHRISTMAS	Midwinter festival originally Saturnalia	Date God's son, Jesus, was born to 'virgin' mother
CIRCUMCISION	Genital mutilation of male babies	Surgery to improve on God's perfect design of man in His Image
CREATIONISM	Unevidenced hypothesis for the origin of everything	True explanation for origin of everything, as given by God's word in Genesis I and II

245

CRUCIFIX	Method of execution	Symbol of Christian faith worn round neck
DARWIN	Proposer of Natural Selection	Son of the Devil
DEAD	Dead	Afterlife in Heaven or Hell
DISCOVERY INSTITUTE	Biased organization funded to back 'god' & the Bible	Research establishment providing evidence for God and the Creation
DIRT	Dirt	Raw material for Adam
EASTER	Spring festival of fertility goddess Eostre – eggs, chicks, bunnies	Weekend God's son Jesus was crucified and resurrected
EVIDENCE	Repeatable, shareable observations	Anything that supports belief in *my* God (not *your* god): sunsets, rainbows and poetry
EVIL	Umbrella of naughtiness	God's special list of bad behaviors (sex)
EVOLUTION	Explanation for the diversity of life on Earth	Atheist plot to scupper Christianity (but not according to the Pope)
FAITH	Unfounded confidence	Alternative form of evidence
FALLEN	Landed awkwardly	Sinful birth of everyone due to Eve eating the 'forbidden fruit'
FISH	Swimming food	To recruit members
FLOOD	God's murder of entire human population, except for Noah's family	Godly Act of cleansing humanity of sin, except for one favored family who repopulated the Earth incestuously
GOD	Mythical being - e.g. Zeus	Real Creator Deity – the one true God

GOSPEL	Genre of choral music with nasal style singers	Biography of Jesus written by one of four unnamed scribes
He/Him	Abuse of rules of English grammar for propaganda purposes	Pronouns capitalized to show proper respect for the one true God and his son Jesus Christ
HEAVENLY	Indulgent - "This is heavenly chocolate"	Like a place where dead Christians live in eternal bliss beside God and the angels
HELL	Unpleasant experience e.g. traffic jam	Place where loving God tortures non-believers for eternity
HERESY	Challenging church values	Punishable questioning of doctrine
HOMOSEXUAL	Gay person	Sodomist needing stoning to death
IMMATERIAL	Not made of matter, unreal	Real, but not as we know it, Jim
INSTITUTE FOR CREATION RESEARCH	Organization funded to back god & the Bible	Academic college that provides proof of Creation
INTELLIGENT DESIGN	Creationism	Whisper, "Can you keep a secret? It's Creationism"
JESUS	Ancient Jewish carpenter's son	God junior, clone of Jehovah.
LEFT HANDED	Left handed	Sinner needing stoning
LIMBO	West Indian dance bending backwards under a pole	Less than hellish place for unbaptised dead babies. Abolished in 2007 by Benedict XVI
MARTYR	Dead person	Hero living in Heaven. In Islam: rewarded with 72 virgins
MIRACLES	Violations of the Laws of Physics	Wonderful events performed by Jesus

247

MORALITY	Evolved social behavior aiding species success	Teachings of Jesus leant to humanity via selected Bible verses
MUSLIM	Follows Islam	Anti-Christ
POLYCOTTON	Crease-free fabric blend	Sinful cloth made of mixed threads
PRAYER	Spell	Message to God
QUR'AN	Islamic Scripture	False Religious book
RAPTURE	Ecstasy	Raised up to heaven
REVELATION	Disclosure	Message from God
RIB	Delicious meat	Raw material for Eve
SACRILEGE	Bogus crime	Violating Christian stuff
SATAN	Mythical being	God's nemesis
SCRIPTURES	Writings	God's word
SHEEP Flock	Wooly animals	Congregation
SHRIMP	Delicious food	Sinful food – big no-no
SIN	Theists' unit of naughtiness	Activities God doesn't like (especially sex)
SLAVERY	Crime against UN Declaration of Human Rights	Menial occupation, once Biblically approved of, currently out of favor
SUPERNATURAL REALM	Unreal fantasy land	A real place outside of, or beyond, reality
TRANSCEND	Surpass limits	Move into the immaterial realm
TRANSUB-STANTIATION	Symbolic cannibalism	Oneness with the body and blood of the Lord
VIRGIN MARY	No man? Do parthenogenesis	Holy Mother of God

248

SUMMARY OF CHAPTER 8

- Centuries of distortion have imbued our language with a Christian bias.
- There is a whole web of fabricated concepts that appear to support each other – 'heaven', 'soul', 'hell', 'evil', 'sin', etc. It's analogous to 'fairyland', 'goblin', 'mermaid', etc.
- There is no evidence for anything 'supernatural', and if we ever find some, it will immediately become natural! Until then it remains merely conceptual.
- Materialism is evidential and has never been falsified.
- Faith, Belief, Confidence and Trust should not be used interchangeably – they each have distinct meanings. Faith is pretending to know something you don't know.

"Propositions that are untestable, unfalsifiable are not worth much"
Carl SAGAN.

"The wise man apportions his belief according to the evidence"
David HUME

Faith means not wanting to know what is true
Friedrich NIETSCHE

9. ANDY: THE THEIST WHO DOESN'T EXIST?

Nobody writes a book to refute 'Afairyism'.

Ask yourself, 'Why not?'

Andy's entire book is an attempt to destroy a similarly imaginary adversary. Yet he only speaks for the prosecution, alleging that his chosen opponent: 'atheism', is an unreasonable 'belief' to hold. Oddly, sometimes he thinks 'atheism' is *a fundamental ideology,* a false 'faith', and sometimes he thinks it is *just personal preferences.* In fact 'atheism' is neither. It is a non-thing. So he is wasting his time.

Andy does not speak in defense of the god hypothesis. He fails to advocate his *own* case. Nowhere does he provide any evidence *for* his god proposition, he only offers argument, experience and made-up stories, none of which are evidence. We are only treated to one side of the coin. Is the other side blank? Ask yourself, why doesn't he provide some evidence for his belief? That would be the only way this question might be settled, after all. *Is Andy the theist who doesn't exist?*

The closest Andy gets to providing evidence is in his Chapter 10 where he poses some questions. He starts by analyzing the meaning of 'proof' in a way that I actually agree with:

'Proof', in the sense that some atheists mean it, brandishing the word around triumphantly like a child with a plastic pirate sword at a fancy dress party, actually exists only in the realm of logic and mathematics. Certainly, I can prove to you that two plus two is four, I can prove to you the law of non-contradiction, but beyond that I can't prove much at all, not even that Richard Dawkins exists.

Well, there's plenty of observational evidence that Richard Dawkins highly probably *does* exist! I've been in the same room as him. But, ignoring the unnecessary attempt at piratical ridicule, Andy is correct: proof only exists in the Conceptual Realm, which includes math and logic, where it is very useful. We can conceive of the absolute certainty that is required for proof, but we have never discovered it. In the Natural Realm we have to be content with evidence and probability. The Natural Realm is *relative* not absolute. Think about that: it means that in reality, evidence is superior to proof, not the other way round, because 'proof' is *not available except in concept*, in other words, in imagination.

Andy goes on to say:

So how might this apply to the God question? Well, in two ways, I believe. First we need to ask the right questions. Rather than sophomoric sound bites (Prove God exists, you dyed-in-the-wool faith-head!) we need to be willing to consider where it points when it is taken together. Among the data we would want to consider would be questions such as why there is something rather than nothing; why the laws of physics appear so finely tuned for life - indeed, why there are laws of nature at all and why mathematics so perfectly describes them; why reason and rationality work, why is it that we find ourselves conscious and able to trust our cognitive processes.

Andy loves using his power of authorship to paint all 'atheists' as insulters but, ignoring the emotive 'faith-head' remark, some of those are very good questions! Andy is giving thought to some unsolved puzzles! However, he is wrong when he asks why we are 'able to trust our cognitive processes'. *We can't.* Our understanding is vulnerable to deception; just look at optical illusions; we merely *think* we can trust our senses and brain. It's a delusion. That's why scientists strive to remove the individual brain from the situation, to be *objective*.

But, it sounds to me as though Dr Bannister is trying to offer those *questions* as evidence for his 'god' (not for any other 'god', of course). I'm trying to be gentle and kind, but the following clause is nonsense, there's no nicer way of saying it:

'Among the data we would want to consider would be questions...'

Questions do not *provide* data: they *request* data. Questions are not answers. Elementary, my dear Dr ~~Watson~~ Bannister.

So, 'why is there something rather than nothing?' Firstly we have to remember that the 'why?' question comes with a presupposition. 'What?' can be answered with 'this', 'where?' with 'there' and 'how?' with 'this way'. They can all be handled with finality, but 'why?' cannot be divorced from the supposition that there is a purpose, reason or intention. That's why the 'why' question triggers a follow up 'why' in an endless chain known as an infinite regression. It is the archetypal example of the Begging the Question Fallacy and there is no evidence that the purposefulness it demands actually exists, except in the case of man-made structures. Christians

253

struggle with this because they like to believe that everything has been caused by their god. I suggest you ask them two questions: "Who designed The Grand Canyon?" and "Whose clever idea was miscarriage?"

But let's *try* to deal with the 'Why is there something rather than nothing?' query. It's just a silly question. For a start, 'nothing' has never been observed. Space is not 'nothing'. It contains light photons, heat and many other wavelengths of the electro-magnetic spectrum, which amount to an average temperature of 3° Kelvin not zero. It also contains thinly dispersed hydrogen atoms and other particles, including virtual particles that pop into and out of existence all the time. It's not even a perfect vacuum. We've tried to make 'nothing' here on Earth and, although we have achieved a much better vacuum than space (we can exclude light for one thing), we can't keep out neutrinos. They pass through everything. So, as far as we know, 'nothing' does not exist – it's just a concept. A better question might be, *"Why is there no evidence for nothing?"* Answer: we don't know.

What about the 'fine-tuning' of the Laws of Physics 'so that' (there's the imagined purposefulness) it's fit for mankind? This is the idea that if the universal physical constants underlying the mathematical description of the universe were slightly different in value, we could not exist. Well, for a start, 99.9%

of the universe is NOT suitable for mankind! We wouldn't last five minutes in the vast majority of it. Yet, given the enormity and diversity of the cosmos, it's hardly surprising that a tiny proportion of it is habitable. Asking 'why?' is a bit like a puddle waking up and wondering how it comes to find itself in its perfectly fitting hollow, and jumping to the conclusion that this depression must have been *made* for it! Our existence enables us to question why and how we exist. If the circumstances were inhospitably different, we wouldn't be here pondering this problem! Maybe the dimensions of the physical constants just ARE... We honestly don't know, but our lack of knowledge is not evidence for *any* 'god', let alone *yours!* It's a quootion not an answer.

Now let's deal with the question of math. Einstein said math is thought and I agree with him. We have invented it. Theists like to claim that math was 'put there by god' for us to discover.

Here are some of the reasons why they are wrong:

• Zero was invented. The Romans had no zero. As explained above, zero (nothing) may not exist; we have never discovered any 'nothing'. "Zero" and "nothing" are mathematical abstractions, concepts, not physical realities when applied to the totality of things we call the universe. We know from history roughly when and where

255

zero was invented and by whom.[78] However, 'nought' *is* a useful conceptual place-holder for a column representing an order of magnitude with no content.

- Infinity was invented (and its chronological cousin, eternity). Even Christian apologist William Lane-Craig acknowledges that it's just an idea. He says that here: http://tinyurl.com/ybqkdlem (at 16 minutes in) Infinity was clarified as a concept in 1874 by George Cantor.[79]

- The very notion of numbers greater than one is a human fabrication. We know that single quanta exist, but putting them into groups and giving the groups names like 'two', 'three' and 'ninety nine' Is just man's conceptualization.

- All numbering systems and nomenclatures have been invented; they are like different languages of math. Early number systems were invented for counting sheep and goats – yan, tan, tethera, etc. We usually count in a Decimal way because our hands have ten digits, but some cultures use the knuckles (joints) of the fingers (not including the thumbs). This Duodecimal system is useful for packing pies or cakes into a reasonably proportioned tray (3 by 4) and it has given us two orders of magnitude - the dozen and the gross. The Babylonians used base sixty. Computers, having only on/off switches, use the Binary system. It is possible to invent a counting system with any base number. Historically, Imperial Units had mixed bases: four farthings to the penny, twelve pennies to the shilling, twenty shillings to the pound, etc. Units of time are still not decimalized. Pigeons can recognize numbers up to seven. Do octopuses count in eights?

- Geometry is based on some preposterous conventions, such as 'a line has length but no width', and 'a point has location but no area'. These are obviously invented concepts with no correspondence to reality. It's unsurprising that perfect proofs are available within Geometry – it's in the Conceptual Realm – we make it up, so we can make it perfect. However, perfection is not available in the Natural Realm due to the lumpy randomness of nature, which denies absoluteness, especially at the quantum scale. There are no perfectly straight lines or perfectly round circles in reality - just magnify to see wobbling irregularity.

- Pi (and some other constants), at least in the math that we humans have invented, will always be merely approximate. There is definitely a relationship between the concept of a circle and the concept of its radius, but math can't describe it accurately. It can only give an approximation. It can give either a *good* approximation - to several decimal places e.g. 3.14159265359 or a *poor* approximation such as 3.142. The accuracy is a matter of choice! We can *choose* different conceptual relationships between the circumference and the radius! The fact that we can *choose* is a clue that math is conceptual, not real, because we can't *actually* choose different measurements for a physical circumference and its radius just to make Pi solve – that would mean altering length and/or shape! Pi is an irrational number.

It helps to think of math as like a transparency that we can lay on top of nature to see if we have constructed a close representation. Using an analogy from chemical photography, sometimes math fits like a negative film onto the positive print of what we observe and sometimes it doesn't. Here's an example – think of sound - it exists as a waveform in the air. A microphone can detect these waves. The microphone's output can be converted into either an analogue electrical waveform, which might match the source accurately, depending on the range of the microphone's sensitivity, or into a digital electrical signal. The digital signal can be a reasonable fit, in the way that a column graph can roughly match a smooth curve, but it can never be a perfect fit. An algorithm has created the digital representation. Even the electrical analogue signal will be steppy given the quantized nature of electrons... Are waves real? Scale might be the explanation here...

Claiming that math is *necessarily* a perfect match for nature is also incorrect. Where it does more or less match, it's because we have honed our math tool to be as good as possible. *Math can perfectly describe concepts* like geometric shapes, so it's

258

great for engineering where we attempt to make perfect shapes in reality, but those smoothly engineered shapes are shown to be rough under magnification. On the other hand *Math can only approximately describe nature.* That's why we have had three models of the 'heavens' – Ptolemy's discredited geocentric spheres, Newton's mathematical description of the Kepler/Copernicus* heliocentric solar system and Einstein's Relativity portrayal of the cosmos. And just think of chaos theory and fuzzy logic...

Can math and logic prove 'god' exists? Well, proof is purely conceptual so, yes, Math and logic could prove 'god' exists *conceptually*. We can conceive of anything, including Humpty Dumpty, but proof is valueless outside of the Conceptual Realm until supported by observational evidence. Investigating reality *could* provide *evidence* (but not proof). However, not only has no evidence for 'god' ever been discovered, but also 'god' is alleged to be 'immaterial' and therefore simply cannot *be* investigated! So 'god' is currently hypothetical, like Tinker Bell and that is how He is likely to remain... Are you satisfied with that?

* 'Copernicus' was a teacher's nightmare word: some clown would always deliberately mishear and shout out, "Copper Knickers!" much to the delight of the class...

Unfortunately, most people think that proof trumps evidence. But proof is conceptual (thought), while evidence is observed in nature (real). So it's really evidence that trumps proof and the same goes for logic. A logical outcome is a thought model that does not necessarily correspond with an evidential conclusion. The problem with proof is that it must be absolute, and absoluteness has never been observed in reality. However, in the Conceptual Realm, we can *imagine* absoluteness and perfection, so we can conceive of proof even if it doesn't exist in the Natural Realm. People need to stop believing that thoughts are automatically true, that's pre-Renaissance thinking! Useful information only comes in the form of *a conceptual model that actually matches observations of reality.*

Now let's tackle 'the difficult question' of consciousness. Many theists like to claim that we are all just bags of molecules and they challengingly ask, "How can that give rise to consciousness?" That's like asking how can the twenty-six letters of the Roman alphabet embody all the meanings in this book! When you realize that one molecule of water on its own cannot be wet, you have to accept that amazing properties can emerge from an assemblage of quite basic units.

See here: http://tinyurl.com/yde2jd5t
and here: http://tinyurl.com/l3scehx

Some theists like to assert that there is a difference between the mind and the brain. This dualism feeds their desire to claim that our 'soul' survives our death and it leads on to their agenda for a heaven and a 'god'. There is no evidence for dualism and, although it's true that scientists don't have an explicit explanation for consciousness yet, progress is being made at steadily increasing speed as new instruments for investigating and simulating the brain are developed. And never forget that our ignorance is not evidence for any 'god'.

To bring you up to date with our current understanding, my report on a 2016 lecture that was given in London by Professor Steven Pinker follows below:

FROM NEURONS TO CONSCIOUSNESS
The link between matter and mind

The more we discover about the brain, the less it seems necessary to invoke the idea of a separate bodiless 'soul' or 'spirit' for human consciousness. The brain is quite suitable for accommodating the mind. Now that we are beginning to understand how it works, we can even build models of its processing mechanisms in silicon circuitry.

Evidence for the coherence of the mind and brain comes in several forms:

1. The brain is an electrical device – electrical stimulation affects thoughts. The evidence is fourfold:

    a) Operations on humans undergoing brain surgery and experiments on monkeys, cats and humans using tiny electrodes to deliver micro jolts (-70 millivolts) to specific brain areas have caused stimulation of limbs and sensations that conscious patients have been able to report as indistinguishable from reality.

b) Disabled patients have been implanted with electrodes that enable them to control robots by thinking.

c) Trans-cranial Magnetic Stimulation, which involves focused magnetic fields on local brain areas, has produced effects altering the perceptions of patients.

d) Functional Nuclear Magnetic Resonance imaging enables the location of brain activity in response to particular thoughts to be identified.

2. The brain is a chemical device – psychoactive drugs can influence it and modulate mood, even cause visions.

3. Stroke or external injury can cause changes in ability or even personality – physical loss of brain functions, of *parts* of the mind.

4. Brain surgery – deliberate ablation of tissue can produce predictable effects on the tendency to suffer epileptic seizures, and severe surgery, such as lobotomy, can produce odd disconnections like the phantom hand.

5. Complexity – the brain is easily complex enough to perform the functions observed in humans – it has 100 billion neurons with 150 trillion connections.

6. Organization – neurons are known to be arranged into AND, OR and NOT gates with, for example, columns in the visual centre aligned to recognize edges. Lateral inhibition of neurons focuses images rather like Photoshop 'sharpening'. Optical Illusions reveal these structures, particularly when neurons become habituated. Networks are hierarchical with more complex feature detectors at

higher levels. A particular spot in one patient's visual centre only fired when he was shown pictures of Jennifer Aniston!

7. Death – when the brain dies, the person is gone.

So the 'Astonishing Hypothesis' is that "Consciousness consists of patterns of information in neural networks"

Research on the brain and its function continues, watch this space...

~~~

Now, please notice that Andy's questions all begin with 'why' and I will respond to them all in general with three more 'why' questions:

- Why should we expect all questions to have an answer?
- Why does Andy think that questions are 'evidence' in support of his preferred explanation? Questions are not answers; ignorance is not knowledge.
- Why did 'god' create a universe that is 99.9% unsuitable for humans? Answer me that one!

We've become accustomed to purpose - in our daily lives we have got used to things having an intention, especially in the developed world where our environment is largely all of our own making. We can look at the road outside and ask why is it there? What is it for? The answer immediately comes back

263

– it's for our vehicles to drive on. I won't bore you with more examples; make up your own! Richard Dawkins deals with this very well – see here: http://tinyurl.com/pqwuuqz

Expecting Andy's 'why' questions to have an answer is an example of the Begging the Question Fallacy. It's assuming that *everything* has a purpose, that everything has been created, like our roads have been, and that there is some sort of a 'creator'[80], a being who did it all. It's a trick question like, "When did you stop beating your wife?" Whichever way you answer it you incriminate yourself! 'Why' is actually a *claim dressed up as a question.* Just because we can frame a 'why' question about a phenomenon doesn't mean it must have a purpose that can be provided as the answer.

What purpose does the blindness-causing nematode eye worm, Loa loa filariasis[81] have, beyond selfishly living and reproducing? Imagining everything is the result of deliberate intention and denying the possibility of randomness is anthropomorphism[82]. Would it make sense to ask "Why did that coin land head uppermost?" No! Because there is no purpose, intention or reason for that to happen. We can't assume that everything has a purpose simply because we humans are purposeful. And, I repeat, unanswered or unanswerable questions are not evidence for *any* 'god', let alone a specifically Christian one.

I have some 'why' questions that I would like to ask of Andy's 'god' if I am ever lucky enough to meet Her! See here:

"Madam, if, as Your earthly sales representatives like to claim, You are omnipotent and You intelligently designed everything for us, including ourselves, and You love us, Your children,

- *Why did You create malaria[90]?*
- *Why did You create Loa loa filariasis[91]?*
- *Why don't You prevent earthquakes?*
- *Why don't You help by digging survivors out of earthquake rubble?*
- *Why didn't You make 'heaven' here on Earth?*
- *Why did You need to sacrifice Your 'son' in a failed attempt to eliminate 'evil'?*
- *Why did You need to drown the entire population except for one family in an earlier failed attempt to eliminate 'evil'?*
- *Come to that, why did You create 'evil' in the first place?*
- *Why did you create miscarriage, cancer and dementia?"*

Obviously I could go on for a very long time in that vein! But the 'why' question that theists never seem to want to even ask, let alone seek an answer to is: "Why did 'god' create the universe?" Of course the reason they keep quiet about this is because it demonstrates the unanswerability of 'why' questions. If they can't answer that 'why' question, I don't see how they can demand that I should answer *their* 'why?' questions.

Earlier in his book Andy was content to accept that there is a category of Things That Are. Remember this:

"On the other hand, it is utterly meaningless to ask whether the colour blue, a small off-duty Slovakian traffic warden, or Richard Dawkins' left foot is 'true'. That would be a bizarre category error. These things are not <u>claims or beliefs</u> and thus do not possess any kind of 'truth value'. <u>They simply are."</u>
(My underlinings)

Back then, Andy used Sweden and Richard Dawkin's left foot as examples of Things That Are. He wasn't asking '*Why* are they?' then, was he. He was content to accept their simple 'areness'. Is his curiosity limited to matters that might suit his pro-'god' agenda? Is he changing his view to whatever suits his bias to support his 'god' presupposition? Is that allowed?

~~~

So, here is my advice for all those who wish to make informed decisions and to avoid being deceived:

1. Question everything, absolutely everything.
2. Don't accept verbal accounts as trustworthy sources of information – people exaggerate and can lie.
3. Don't even trust books or documents – they need verifying by checking their claims.
4. Don't trust those who claim to be eye-witnesses.
5. Don't even trust your own senses, they can be deceived.
6. Don't follow the majority view without questioning – everyone once thought iron ships would sink.
7. Don't accept arguments as evidence.
8. Don't imagine that logic can turn a hypothesis into a conclusion – it's purely conceptual and has no automatic correspondence with reality.
9. Demand repeatable observations as the only valid form of evidence (try to get actual measurements).
10. Don't be fooled by evidence that supports physical structures when the claim is about an event or action.
11. Don't consider faith to be any good for anything.
12. Be doubly skeptical about extraordinary claims that defy the laws of Physics or postulate unnatural realms.
13. Remember that hypotheses are not conclusions and that questions are not answers.

And here is the current state of our understanding of the 'fundamental questions':

1. How did the universe come to exist?

We don't know, but we are investigating a few hypotheses.

2. How is it that the Earth is so suitable for life?

Because it has the right temperature, gravity and composition.

3. How did life begin?

We don't know, but we are investigating a few hypotheses.

4. How did the amazing diversity of life come about?

It evolved as a result of natural selection.

5. What is consciousness?

We don't know yet, but we are developing techniques that might help us to find out. Especially fNMR and PET

6. How is it that math describes reality so well?

Because we have invented it to enable the modeling of explanations and to play with numbers.

7. How can we trust science when it's based on the assumption of materiality?

Because it has been shown to work.

8. Why is a hypothesis not a truth?

Consult a dictionary.

9. What does 'Theory' mean in science?

Consult a Science dictionary.

10. Why do you want there to be a 'god'?

Because even an incorrect answer is less scary than ignorance.

So what about

Part Two: The Construction of a Rational Worldview?

Well, if you've read this far you should know how to recognize evidence and how to be skeptical about claims. That's a science teacher's job done. I don't want to tell you what to think; just use the thinking tools to investigate reality and make up your own mind about how things work.

A good teacher shows you where to look but doesn't tell you what to see.

10. FINALE

I enjoy writing – living in a house full of people it's often the only chance I get to express myself without interruption! Thankfully, social media have enormously improved our opportunities to put our points of view – you can't be shouted down or interrupted online, but you can still be ignored...

This particular book has been easy to write because I've been able to focus on Christianity, since Andy Bannister, whose book The Atheist Who Didn't Exist inspired this response, is a Christian. My earlier book on this subject, Godbuster, attempted to deal with religions in general although most of the examples given referred to Biblical notions, which enabled Christians to bleat that they were being unfairly targeted, despite my explanation in the Introduction.

It might be worth mentioning that my 'targeting' takes the harmless form of writing, whereas Christians have physically targeted scientists like Galileo[92] (imprisoned) and Giordano Bruno[93] (tortured and killed) for merely contradicting Biblical claims about the universe, which we now know were completely false. The Bible clearly expounds Ptolemy's[94] erroneous belief that the 'firmament' (sky) was a series of clear concentric glasslike spheres carrying the moon, planets and stars around our world. The conflict with this religious doctrine is why Bruno's more accurate heliocentric model of the solar system was considered heresy and 'therefore' he was 'deserving' of death.

However, there *is* a big problem with writing refutations of Christian apologia: it's the difficulty of trying to disentangle the mass of erroneous assumptions that populate almost every sentence. Some Christians can't string four words together without making baloney! There are just so many falsehoods originating in the belief that the Bible is essentially correct, and from all of that false information a lot of misconceptions derive. The result is that Christian writing takes the form of a theistic web that cannot be unraveled linearly because so many of the words we need to use have peculiarly religious connotations that require clearing up en route. You saw, at the beginning of this book, that it took me *eleven pages* just to deal with the title of Andy's book and one of his sentences!

After two millennia of infection, Western culture has become so thoroughly contaminated with Christian mythology that the believers have recruited our very language as an ally to their 'god' and a saboteur to non-belief. We can hardly say anything without referencing Christianity! Thank 'heavens' for quotation marks to indicate false concepts; it's a good job there is no risk of speech marks running out! Also, thank 'god' for *Notes*, which enable me to keep to a reasonably logical thread in the run of the text without getting sidetracked into other issues – just go to the Notes to see the ramifications.

A-choo! *Bless you!* That's an expression originally intended to encourage your 'spirit' that you had just 'sneezed out' through your nostrils, to re-enter your body! There is no escape from language contaminated by 'god'!

You'll have noticed that I don't use a capital 'G' for 'god'. I deliberately *don't* capitalize it because 'god' is not a *name*; it's an ordinary noun like 'goblin'. Capitalizing 'god' is tantamount to naming your dog, 'Dog'! Isn't it sneaky of the Christians to have commandeered the word 'god' to refer exclusively to *their* 'God' when there are thousands of other 'gods' it ought to be available to apply to? On the other hand, 'Zeus' *is* a name, so is 'Allah'[95], 'Yahweh'[96], 'Jesus'[97] and 'Ganesha'[98], so consequently they *are* entitled to an upper case initial.

What would you think if I wrote about Darwin and always referred to Him with a capital 'H'? Wouldn't you think I was biased in His favor and was trying to boost His importance in your eyes? Isn't that just a transparent ruse? It's propaganda, isn't it? Why would an omnipotent being have to stoop to such pathetic measures as abusing the conventions of English grammar by capitalizing *pronouns* just to gain public stature? Darwin doesn't need me to do that for Him, does He! Come to

272

that, why does an omnipotent Creator Deity need puny human representatives at all?

Take the sex of 'god' as another example. I often refer to 'god' as 'She' or 'Her' in order to make the point that sexing 'god' is an anthropomorphic assumption. Surely, out of the two sexes, the female is the one most involved in birth, so don't the feminine pronouns describe a creator who allegedly delivered the universe much better than the masculine ones?

The sex of 'god' wasn't so much of a problem back in the old days of Nature 'gods' like rivers and volcanoes - they are obviously sexless. Sex only became a serious issue with the invention of manlike 'gods'. You can't have a humanoid without addressing the question of which sex it is. But here's the thing: why would the one and only *eternal* creator deity need genitalia? Is She going to reproduce? Why? She's not going to die and need replacing is She... Reproduce *with whom?* It must be impossibly difficult to find a suitable 'godly' partner in a cosmos that only has *one* 'god'! Has She been frustrated for millennia or has She secretly already given birth to offspring? Did She marry or were they conceived in 'sin'? Maybe She's a virgin who was impregnated by a deity from the Superdupernatural Realm? If so, where *are* all the little 'godlets'? Or has She been using contraception (Roman Catholic shock horror)! Perhaps She's *homosexual!* (Baptist

273

shock horror)! Maybe She has passed the menopause. Would an 'Omnipotent Being' permit that to happen to Herself? Is She perhaps, gasp, horror, *barren?* Ask yourself these questions. *Sexuality is about reproduction, which is a mechanism to combat mortality; an immortal eternal god should have no need of it.* Such nonsense!

(Did you know Yahweh had a wife? 'Asherah' was quietly edited out of the Torah! See here: http://tinyurl.com/jnkc7h9)

Or has Jehovah been made masculine simply because men had control over society when the monotheistic 'god' was invented? Bible authors, going by their own words, were obviously misogynists; it would have been demeaning for them to bow down to a *'goddess'.* Surely that's the reason 'god' was created in the image of a *man.* What we know about society in those days suggests that men wanted to subjugate women, so isn't that why they made 'god' a 'Him'?

This is so obvious that I can't understand why it has not become *a reason to disbelieve,* especially among women who, bizarrely, still make up the largest proportion of every dwindling congregation in the UK! Women have had to struggle to become clergy in the Anglican denomination and the Pope says they will never become priests. Why are women in Christianity at all? Do they *want* to be considered inferior? Are any feminists believers? If so, why?

Come to that, Jesus is commonly depicted as ethnically Caucasian and yet ethnic Africans, who were historically traded as slaves (as condoned in the Bible) by the very white men who brought them Christianity, are often the most devout followers of a pale-skinned Jesus!

It seems to me that some people have only to get a couple of hypothetical assumptions fixed in their heads as 'truths' in infancy and then they are prepared to construct a whole belief system, based on falsehoods or mere hypotheses, which they are willing to defend vehemently. Joining an organized religion increases the commitment by many techniques. Members are peer-pressured into adopting the symbols of belonging – the Christianization of life's events, the dress code, the acceptable haircut, the diet, the constant expectation of making 'offerings', the subconscious language of 'god bless you', 'god willing', in some sects even to the denial of life-saving blood transfusions to their children.

Given that the existence of a god (or many gods) is merely hypothetical, the scientific thing to do would be to evaluate the probability of the god proposition being correct. In fact, this cannot be done on a comparison of the evidence for and against, because the 'god' hypothesis has *no* repeatedly observable evidence at all. Logically, that makes 'god' *infinitely improbable*. The discovery of evidence would instantly overrule this logic. Unfortunately, such a discovery is precluded by the assertion that She is undetectably immaterial!

So, like all the other apologists, in the absence of fact, Andy has had to turn to fiction. He writes stories rather better than most, but even *he* can't give them the power of evidence. In their attempt to bolster their non-evidential claims, apologists are prepared to resort to all sorts of stories. For example, leading anti-theist Christopher Hitchens predicted, just before he died, that rumors would be circulated alleging he had a 'death-bed' conversion to Christianity and, sure enough, a scurrilous author is cashing in on a book claiming exactly that! Christopher Hitchens pointed out that *before we developed astronomy we believed in astrology and before we developed chemistry we believed in alchemy; by the same token we now have no reason to follow religion and should ditch faith if we want to make progress in life.* What is the value of belief?

The growing number of ex-clerics, and would-be ex-clerics who are still trapped in their livelihoods as priests or pastors, is testament to the fact that the Christian edifice is a house of cards on the brink of collapsing. Support organizations now exist in the USA[99] and UK[100] to help these brave apostatized, or apostatizing, religious professionals to repurpose their lives and find different employment, but little can be done to help rebuild their social circles, from which they will be ostracized by the unthinking. Such is the social pressure of membership of a faith.

Becoming faithless from the position of a publicly declared religious official is a psychological struggle with one's own mind. Leaving must be like adopting a new identity in middle age following the completion of a sentence for a murder committed in childhood! Overnight, ex-clergy can dispense with the dog collar (ASBO tag equivalent), wear ordinary clothes, have a conventional haircut/shave and eat pork on Friday! The entrapment shibboleths, which they were subjected to previously, suddenly fall away, but they leave nothing behind...

Back in an age of presupposing a 'maker', Bertrand Russell said,

"'Who made me?' cannot be answered, since it immediately suggests the further question, 'Who made 'god'?' This led me to abandon the 'First Cause' argument, and to become an atheist."

I contend that a theist's life path often goes like this:
- Born innocent and ignorant,
- Inducted into a denomination by family and tribe,

- Then having to make a conscious, informed decision to abandon that faith and all the associated social implications later in life.

It's a deconversion rather than an adoption of 'atheism' – like growing out of belief in Santa Claus and, just like in that process, rationalism offers nothing to replace the myth. That's why there is no ideology of Asantaclausism.

Let me put you on the spot: suppose you know someone who has a calcified aortic valve. Would you recommend him to go with the evidential cure of having the valve surgically replaced, which might extend his life by fifteen years or more, or would you advise him to go with the treatment suggested by your faith, whatever that is? Prayer? Sacrifice? Pilgrimage? Worship? What if it was *you* with the damaged heart valve? Would you go to the hospital for cardiac surgery or to the church for superstition? Actually, you *do* know someone who was in that situation – me! Guess which route I took... I'm ok now, thanks for asking, and yes, I'm enjoying my 'afterlife'!

THE RANT:

Why do I focus on religion? After all, I don't support astrology or homeopathy either... Well, I do it because, although other forms of woo might victimize their own believers, they are less harmful to humanity in general since they don't cause ongoing conflict and strife down the generations in the way that faiths do. Why don't they? Because few people *really* believe in the unscientific superstitious endeavors of homeopathy (it's just been unfunded by the UK Health Service) and astrology, and they don't have a fervent mission to indoctrinate their children.

But, *Belief in a 'god' is genuinely dangerous. Beware of men who have dogmatic certainty about their beliefs. Particularly beware of ill-educated young fundamentalists – they are too easily radicalized, they want a 'cause' and they are too reckless.* Non-belief is the only credible, rational, benign, and humanitarian option.

In this book I have tried to argue that scientific method, resting on the unfalsified assumption of materialism, is the single unchallenged and best means for discovering information. Although that *doesn't* make it:

a)   All knowing,
b)   Absolutely certain, or
c)   A religious doctrine to join for worship.

The fact is, in practice we treat scientific discoveries as *'true'* and not requiring active believing. On the other hand, even faith *leaders* rightly regard belief systems based on improbable, untestable, hypothetical gods *as extremely dubious and in need of constant reaffirming.* Disbelief is reciprocal. Christians disbelieve Islam. Muslims disbelieve Christianity. Christians and Muslims disbelieve Judaism. Jews disbelieve Christianity and Islam. All three disbelieve Hinduism, Buddhism, Sikhism, Satanism and Scientology. Disbelief in the religions of others is the normal condition. We are all 'others'. Therefore beliefs are all unbelievable.

Christianity is a burden on humanity. Asserting that we have been born in 'original sin' leads to a mental attitude of victimhood, of low self-esteem, of unworthiness, which is instilled from infancy. It fosters a demeaning need to 'bend the knee' in submission to a supposed supernatural, omnipotent being who allegedly has the malicious power to torture dead non-believers for eternity! (Yet, contradictorily, He 'loves' His human 'children' allegedly!)

Such belief systems lead to an exaggerated view of the capability of authority (which is useful for those in power) and, consequently, a paranoid feeling of oppression by 'the elite' in the minds of followers. This spills over into a general suspicion of experts and a demonization of the leaders of *all* organizations from elected governments to police forces and commercial enterprises. It imposes a persecution complex, which leads to conspiracy theorizing in attempts to confirm one's warped impression of the frightfulness of life and the fear of going to 'hell'. This deliberate destruction of individuals' self-confidence is like the mental abuse that some wives experience at the hands of a brutal husband and it should similarly be grounds for separation or divorce from religion. Christianity is a psychologically damaging means of mass behavior control for the financial benefit of its organizers. Islam is even worse, being involved in physical harm like the cutting off of hands.

If you ever see me about to be duped into performing a malicious act on people simply because they don't share our beliefs, I want you to warn me,

If you ever see me about to be conned into handing over money to someone who claims to be the earthly representative of a supernatural being, I want you to warn me.

If you ever see me about to be deceived into thinking that homosexuals should be punished for 'sin', I want you to warn me.

If you ever see me about to be groomed into thinking that women are inferior and should be submissive to men, I want you to warn me.

If you ever see me about to be threatened into submitting to the control of a self-proclaimed earthly representative of an unevidenced being, I want you to warn me.

Warning me of those deceptions would be a moral and humane thing to do, *that's why I am doing it for you.*

~~~

I suggest that the de-theistication of planet Earth should begin by attempting to persuade *moderates* that their belief is unimportant. Not only are they likely to be easier to convince than extremists, but also, reducing their numbers would remove the claim of massive numerical support that gives fundamentalists bogus 'justification' for their atrocities. Additionally, the more breeding-age adults we can enlighten and release from religion, the fewer children will be indoctrinated in future and non-belief will gain from positive feedback over the generations; humanity will drift towards non-belief. I submit that this is a highly moral and worthy enterprise for the betterment of mankind.

SIXTEEN PITFALLS FOR THEISTS TO AVOID

1. Expecting certainty and considering ignorance to be evidence

2. Mistaking argument or proof for evidence. They are in the Conceptual Realm.

3. Mistaking personal experience/revelation/dream for evidence – it can't be shared.

4. Accepting testimony or witness as evidence - it's tainted by the agenda of the teller, whether first hand or hearsay.

5. Accepting archeological remains as evidence for historic *events*.

6. Accepting written accounts (books) as evidence - Nullius in verba – take nobody's word for it, neither written nor spoken; text needs verifying.

7. Accepting anecdotes (single observations) as evidence.

8. Accepting Hypotheses as evidence.

9. Accepting claims as evidence.

10. Conflating observations with conclusions.

11. Mistaking a hypothesis for a Theory or Conclusion.

12. Imagining that a hypothesis can be supported by another hypothesis.

13. Assigning beliefs with importance: they are just choices.

14. Failing to question parents, pastors and priests.

15. Demonizing people who don't belong to your faith.

16. Inducting your children into your faith before they can make an informed decision for themselves.

The good news is that theists, instead of just fighting each other as they have done for centuries, now feel the need to target 'atheism', which shows that they perceive it as a threat: non-belief is on the rise.

Caught You!

I'm aware that some of you browsing this book will have opened it at the back pages. Yes, we've all done that! Why? Because we want to shortcut to the dénouement, that's why!

Are you are one of those? Maybe you're a journalist who is short of time and is seeking to paint me as a 'militant athcist' in order to sensationalize your review into a sound-bite for your audience's delectation?

If so, I urge you to read from the beginning to comprehend my thesis in full. Be fair; allow me to develop my argument; please don't misrepresent me with a cherry-picked quote!

Ok, I give in, the purpose of this book is to get people to re-evaluate belief; it should be regarded as trivial, of monumental unimportance.

Notes:

1. I'm also a father, grandfather and an erstwhile minor politician.

2. **Skeptics in the Pub** is an informal social club designed to promote fellowship and networking among skeptics, critical-thinkers, and other like-minded individuals. It provides an opportunity for skeptics and rationalists to talk, share ideas in a casual atmosphere, and discuss whatever topical issues come to mind. It allows participants to have fun while promoting skepticism, science, and rationality. The usual format of meetings includes an invited speaker who gives a talk on a specific topic, followed by a question-and-answer session. Other meet-ups include debates, movies or informal socials, with no fixed agenda. The groups usually meet once a month at a public venue, most often a local pub. There are now more than 100 different "SitP" groups running around the world. From Wikipedia.

3. Throughout this book I'm using 'conclusions' in the scientific sense of an outcome validated by evidence in the form of shareable repeatable observations. Logical 'conclusions' are in the Conceptual Realm and therefore are very different beasts with much lower significance.

4. Throughout this book I'm using 'hypothesis' in the scientific sense of untested assumption, tentative explanation, conceptualization or informed guess. Technically, a hypothesis should be testable.

5. This is a reference to the story by Spanish author, Miguel de Cervantes, about a man who reads so many chivalric romances that he loses his sanity and decides to set out to revive chivalry, undo wrongs, and bring justice to the world, under the name *Don Quixote de la Mancha*. He famously rides his 'stallion' (often depicted as a donkey) in an attempt to lance an enemy windmill!

6. Yes, 'atheistophobia' is a real word! It's a new term for the irrational hatred or fear of 'atheists'.
   See - https://en.wikipedia.org/wiki/Discrimination_against_atheists

7. The Mind Projection Fallacy occurs when someone thinks that the way they see the world reflects the way the world really is, so they assume everyone experiences the same reaction as them.

8. 'Atheism' - late 16th century: from French *athéisme*, from Greek *atheos*, from *a* - 'without' + *theos* - 'god'

9. The 'Jehovah Witnesses' is a Christian sect that believes the destruction of the present world system at 'Armageddon' is imminent, and that the establishment of God's kingdom over the earth is the only solution for all of the problems faced by humanity. They are best known for their door-to-door preaching, distributing literature such as *The Watchtower* and *Awake!*, and for refusing military service and blood transfusions. Much fun can be had by inviting Jehovah Witnesses into your house and asking them "Ah, you're offering me the *truth*, are you? Which 'truth' do you mean? Objective or subjective truth? Absolute or relative truth? How can we be sure if it's *really* 'true'? What actually *makes* a proposition 'true'? What test can we apply to verify it?

10. False equivalence is a logical fallacy in which two opposing arguments appear to be logically equivalent when in fact they are not. This fallacy is categorized as a fallacy of inconsistency.

11. There are two versions of the Commandments in the Bible with different numbering. 'Thou shall not kill' is number six in one account and number 5 in the Jewish Talmud version. Counting all the statements separately totals thirteen.

    https://en.wikipedia.org/wiki/Ten_Commandments

12. Religions may have promoted cohesion amongst the members of small separate tribes early in human history but, today, as a result of population growth they cause animosity and friction between different overlapping cultures.

13. Incidentally, 'god' was a genocidal dictator on more than one occasion, if you believe the Bible.

    See http://skepticsannotatedbible.com/1sam/15.html

14. Maybe we *should* send out 'atheist missionaries' and become rich!

15. The Straw Man Fallacy is a common form of argument and is an informal fallacy based on giving the impression of refuting an opponent's argument, while actually refuting an argument that was not advanced by that opponent.

16. Neil Gaiman said. 'A book is a dream that you hold in your hand.'

17. Russell's teapot, sometimes called the celestial teapot or cosmic teapot, is an analogy, coined by the philosopher Bertrand Russell, to illustrate that the philosophic burden of proof lies upon a person making scientifically unfalsifiable claims, rather than shifting the burden of disproof to others. Wikipedia

18. There are two dictionary definitions of immaterial - either 'not consisting of matter: incorporeal', or 'of no substantial consequence: unimportant', but that's not what theists mean by the word. They apply it to a hypothetical realm that is outside of reality and is occupied by an invisible, undetectable super being who created everything. For them, 'immaterial' means an undetectable type of reality. This is pure speculation of course.

19. According to the Stanford Encyclopedia of Philosophy, there are two classes of statements – *beliefs, which most analytic philosophers agree are dispositional, affirmative attitudes towards propositions or states of affairs.* By 'dispositional' they mean a proposition that is currently under consideration (and is known in science as a hypothesis). The other class of statements is *premises*, which consist of *concrete events or facts, which presumably cannot be false.*

20. USA Secretary of Defense, Donald Rumsfeld said, *"Reports that say that something hasn't happened are always interesting to me, because as we know, there are known knowns; there are things we know we know. We also know there are known unknowns; that is to say we know there are some things we do not know. But there are also unknown unknowns – the ones we don't know we don't know. And if one looks throughout the history of our country and other free countries, it is the latter category that tends to be the difficult one."* Source: Department of Defense news briefing, February 12, 2002

21. It's regrettable that some authorities now require us to declare our ethnicity. It gives an undeserved air of importance to race and fixes our classification by the triviality of skin color. It's nearly as bad as the old South African apartheid system with the only improvement being WE

get to specify instead of THEM. I wonder how many generations are necessary to drop our ancestral origins? We won't stop racism until we can agree to ignore skin color. In terms of DNA, skin color is due to one nucleotide out of 3,000,000,000 in the human genome – an insignificant difference.

22. Gravity is the weakest of the four fundamental forces. It is proportional to mass, infinite in range and diminishes with the square of distance. Recently gravity waves were detected. 'Graviton' particles remain hypothetical and undiscovered.

23. Bankers' best guesses about the Vatican's wealth put it at $10 billion to $15 billion. Of this wealth, Italian stockholdings alone run to $1.6 billion, 15% of the value of listed shares on the Italian market. The Vatican has big investments in banking, insurance, chemicals, steel, construction, real estate. Dividends help pay for Vatican expenses and charities such as assisting 1,500,000 children and providing some measure of food and clothing to 7,000,000 needy Italians. Unlike ordinary stockholders, the Vatican pays no taxes on this income. From Time magazine.

24. In argumentation theory, an **argumentum ad populum** (Latin for "appeal to the people") is a fallacious argument that concludes that a proposition is true because many or most people believe it: "If many believe so, it is so." This type of argument is known by several names, including appeal to the masses, appeal to belief, appeal to the majority, appeal to democracy, appeal to popularity, argument by consensus, consensus fallacy, authority of the many, and the bandwagon fallacy (also known as a vox populi), and in Latin as *argumentum ad numerum* ("appeal to the number"), and *consensus gentium* ("agreement of the clans"). It is also the basis of a number of social phenomena, including communal reinforcement and the bandwagon effect. From Wikipedia.

25. A study, The Freethought Report 2013, was issued by the International Humanist and Ethical Union (IHEU), a global body uniting atheists, agnostics and other religious skeptics, to mark United Nations' Human Rights Day.

"This report shows that the overwhelming majority of countries fail to respect the rights of atheists and freethinkers although they have signed U.N agreements to treat all citizens equally," said IHEU President Sonja Eggerickx.

The study covered all 192 member states in the world body and involved lawyers and human rights experts looking at statute books, court records and media accounts to establish the global situation.

A first survey of 60 countries last year showed just seven where death, often by public beheading, is the punishment for either blasphemy or apostasy - renouncing belief or switching to another religion which is also protected under U.N. accords.

But this year's more comprehensive study showed six more, bringing the full list to Afghanistan, Iran, Malaysia, Maldives, Mauritania, Nigeria, Pakistan, Qatar, Saudi Arabia, Somalia, Sudan, United Arab Emirates and Yemen.

In others, like India in a recent case involving a leading critic of religion, humanists say police are often reluctant or unwilling to investigate murders of atheists carried out by religious fundamentalists.

Across the world, the report said, "there are laws that deny atheists' right to exist, revoke their citizenship, restrict their right to marry, obstruct their access to public education, prevent them working for the state...."

Criticism of religious faith or even academic study of the origins of religions is frequently treated as a crime and can be equated to the capital offence of blasphemy. REUTERS

26. "When the facts change, I change my mind. What, sir, do you do?" John Maynard Keynes.

"If the evidence shows I am wrong, I will change my mind. Changing your mind when the evidence changes is a sign of intelligence." Prof Edzard Ernst.

27. Science is a probability system so all knowledge is provisional and nothing is sacred, although any concept that has achieved the status of Theory is so well founded on evidence it should stand the test of time. Having said that, when Theories are challenged, they tend to be

improved marginally rather than completely falsified. This happened in the early twentieth century when Einstein's Relativity Theory pushed Newton's Theory of Gravity off the top spot. Newton's Laws are still accurate enough to program spacecraft to navigate to the moons of the outer planets of the solar system. There is no sign that certainty actually exists but evidence can be so strong that the information it supports no longer requires active believing.

28. Not much! A belief is a proposition about which it is possible to hold different opinions. They are both dubious.

29. On the afternoon of 9 October 2012, Malala Yousafzai boarded her school bus in the northwest Pakistani district of Swat. A gunman asked for her by name, then pointed a pistol at her and fired three shots. One bullet hit the left side of Yousafzai's forehead, travelled under her skin through the length of her face, and went into her shoulder. In the days immediately following the attack, she remained unconscious and in critical condition, but later her condition improved enough for her to be sent to the Queen Elizabeth Hospital in Birmingham, England, for intensive rehabilitation. Wikipedia

30. 'Heavenly' is one of those words that has a theistic meaning and a secular meaning. Non-believers use it to mean sublime, delightful or enchanting; believers use it to mean the habitation of 'god' and the 'angels'.

31. 'Supernatural' means of, or relating to, existence outside the natural world. It is non-evidential.

32. 'Transcend' means 'surpass' to secularists but theists take it to mean to exist above and independent of material experience or the universe: "One never can see the thing in itself, because the mind does not transcend phenomena" (Hilaire Belloc).

33. 'Righteous' is a theistic word meaning characterized by, proceeding from, or in accordance with accepted standards of morality, justice, or uprightness; virtuous: a righteous man.

34. 'Afterlife' - A life or existence believed to follow death (!)

35. 'Scientism' is a word introduced by theists for the purpose of

291

denigrating science. They use it to mean the application of, or belief in, the uncritical application of scientific or quasi-scientific methods to inappropriate fields of study or investigation. It is intended to misrepresent science as a 'religion' with values and principles and promotes the misguided notion that science is a subject rather than a process.

36. In philosophy, the **brain in a vat** (alternatively known as **brain in a jar**) is a scenario used in a variety of thought experiments intended to draw out certain features of our ideas of knowledge, reality, truth, mind, consciousness and meaning. It is an updated version of René Descartes' Evil Demon thought experiment originated by Gilbert Harman. Common to many science fiction stories, it outlines a scenario in which a mad scientist, machine, or other entity might remove a person's brain from the body, suspend it in a vat of life-sustaining liquid, and connect its neurons by wires to a supercomputer which would provide it with electrical impulses identical to those the brain normally receives. According to such stories, the computer would then be simulating reality (including appropriate responses to the brain's own output) and the "disembodied" brain would continue to have perfectly normal conscious experiences, such as those of a person with an embodied brain, without these being related to objects or events in the real world. Wikipedia

37. M C Escher's art work features mathematical objects and operations including impossible objects, explorations of infinity, reflection, symmetry, perspective, truncated and stellated polyhedra, hyperbolic geometry, and tessellations. Although Escher considered that he had no mathematical ability, he interacted with mathematicians George Pólya, Roger Penrose, and Harold Coxeter, read mathematical papers by these authors and by the crystallographer Friedrich Haag, and conducted his own original research into tessellation. Wikipedia.

38. The overall process of the scientific method involves making conjectures (hypotheses), deriving predictions from them as logical consequences, and then carrying out experiments based on those

predictions. Although procedures vary from one field of inquiry to another, identifiable features are frequently shared in common between them. A hypothesis is a conjecture, based on knowledge obtained while formulating the question. The hypothesis might be very specific or it might be broad. Scientists then test hypotheses by conducting experiments. Under modern interpretations, a scientific hypothesis must be falsifiable, implying that it is possible to identify a possible outcome of an experiment that conflicts with predictions deduced from the hypothesis; otherwise, the hypothesis cannot be meaningfully tested. Wikipedia.

39. **Philae** (/ˈfaɪliː/ or /ˈfiːleɪ/) is a robotic European Space Agency lander that accompanied the *Rosetta* spacecraft until it separated to land on comet 67P/Churyumov–Gerasimenko, ten years and eight months after departing Earth. On 12 November 2014, *Philae* touched down on the comet, but it bounced when its anchoring harpoons failed to deploy and a thruster designed to hold the probe to the surface did not fire. After bouncing off the surface twice, *Philae* achieved the first-ever "soft" (nondestructive) landing on a comet nucleus, although the lander's final, uncontrolled touchdown left it in a non-optimal location and orientation. Despite the landing problems, the probe's instruments obtained the first images from a comet's surface. Several of the instruments on *Philae* made the first direct analysis of a comet, sending back data that will be analysed to determine the composition of the surface. Wikipedia. Update: the isotope makeup of the comet's ice is different from the water found on Earth.

40. **Poliomyelitis**, often called **polio** or **infantile paralysis**, is an infectious disease caused by the poliovirus. In about 0.5% of cases there is muscle weakness resulting in an inability to move. This can occur over a few hours to a few days. The weakness most often involves the legs but may less commonly involve the muscles of the head, neck and diaphragm. Many but not all people fully recover. In those with muscle weakness about 2% to 5% of children and 15% to 30% of adults die. Another 25% of people have minor symptoms such as fever and a sore

throat and up to 5% have headache, neck stiffness and pains in the arms and legs. The disease is preventable with the polio vaccine; however, a number of doses are required for it to be effective. The US Centers for Disease Control and Prevention recommends polio vaccination boosters for travelers and those who live in countries where the disease is occurring. Once infected there is no specific treatment. In 2015 polio affected less than 100 people, down from 350,000 cases in 1988. In 2014 the disease was only spreading between people in Afghanistan, Nigeria, and Pakistan. In 2015 Nigeria had stopped the spread of wild poliovirus but it reoccurred in 2016. It is hoped that vaccination efforts and early detection of cases will result in global eradication of the disease by 2018. Wikipedia

41. **Smallpox** was an infectious disease caused by either of two virus variants, *Variola major* and *Variola minor*. The last naturally occurring case of smallpox (*Variola minor*) was diagnosed on 26 October 1977. Infection with smallpox is focused in small blood vessels of the skin and in the mouth and throat before disseminating. In the skin it results in a characteristic maculopapular rash and, later, raised fluid-filled blisters. *V. major* produced a more serious disease and had an overall mortality rate of 30–35 percent. *V. minor* caused a milder form of disease (also known as **alastrim**, **cottonpox**, **milkpox**, **whitepox**, and **Cuban itch**) which killed about 1 percent of its victims. Long-term complications of *V. major* infection included characteristic scars, commonly on the face, which occur in 65–85 percent of survivors. Blindness resulting from corneal ulceration and scarring, and limb deformities due to arthritis and osteomyelitis were less common complications, seen in about 2–5 percent of cases. The disease killed an estimated 400,000 Europeans annually during the closing years of the 18th century (including five reigning monarchs), and was responsible for a third of all blindness. Of all those infected, 20–60 percent—and over 80 percent of infected children—died from the disease. Smallpox was responsible for an estimated 300–500 million deaths during the 20th century. As recently as 1967, the World Health Organization (WHO) estimated that 15

million people contracted the disease and that two million died in that year. After vaccination campaigns throughout the 19th and 20th centuries, the WHO certified the global eradication of smallpox in 1979. Smallpox is one of two infectious diseases to have been eradicated, the other being rinderpest, which was declared eradicated in 2011. Wikipedia

42. **Rinderpest** (also **cattle plague** or **steppe murrain**) was an infectious viral disease of cattle, domestic buffalo, and some other species of even-toed ungulates, including buffaloes, large antelope and deer, giraffes, wildebeests, and warthogs. The disease was characterized by fever, oral erosions, diarrhea, lymphoid necrosis, and high mortality. Death rates during outbreaks were usually extremely high, approaching 100% in immunologically naïve populations. Rinderpest was mainly transmitted by direct contact and by drinking contaminated water, although it could also be transmitted by air. After a global eradication campaign, the last confirmed case of rinderpest was diagnosed in 2001. On 14 October 2010, the United Nations Food and Agriculture Organization (FAO) announced that field activities in the decades-long, worldwide campaign to eradicate the disease were ending, paving the way for a formal declaration in June 2011 of the global eradication of rinderpest. On 25 May 2011, the World Organisation for Animal Health announced the free status of the last eight countries not yet recognized (a total of 198 countries were now free of the disease), officially declaring the eradication of the disease. In June 2011, the United Nations FAO confirmed the disease was eradicated, making rinderpest only the second disease in history to be fully wiped out, following smallpox. Wikipedia

43. Theory of mind is the ability to attribute mental states—beliefs, intents, desires, pretence, knowledge, etc.—to oneself and others and to understand that others have beliefs, desires, intentions, and perspectives that are different from one's own. Wikipedia.

44. The ontological argument for 'god' was first proposed by Anselm of Canterbury in his 1078 work *Proslogion*. Anselm defined 'god' as "that

than which nothing greater can be conceived", and argued that this being must exist in the mind, even in the mind of the person who denies the existence of 'god'. He suggested that, if the greatest possible being exists in the mind, it must also exist in reality. If it only exists in the mind, then an even greater being must be possible — one which exists both in the mind and in reality. Therefore, this greatest possible being must exist in reality. Wikipedia

That's nonsense of course, since the mind can conceive of all sorts of things that don't exist in reality: read Alice in Wonderland if you doubt me. But, if you want a stronger defeater, just substitute your nice 'god' with a satanic beast in the argument. Do you want the 'proof' to be used for him? 'Evil god' anyone?

45. In science, a **theory** is a well-substantiated explanation of some aspect of the natural world that is acquired through the scientific method and repeatedly tested and confirmed, preferably using a written, pre-defined, protocol of observations and experiments. Scientific theories are the most reliable, rigorous, and comprehensive form of scientific knowledge.

It is important to note that the definition of a "scientific theory" (often ambiguously contracted to "theory" for the sake of brevity, including in this page) as used in the disciplines of science is significantly different from, and in contrast to, the common vernacular usage of the word "theory". As used in everyday non-scientific speech, "theory" implies that something is an unsubstantiated and speculative guess, conjecture, idea, or, hypothesis; such a usage is the opposite of the word 'theory' in science. These different usages are comparable to the differing, and often opposing, usages of the term "prediction" in science (less ambiguously called a "scientific prediction") versus "prediction" in vernacular speech, denoting a mere hope.

The strength of a scientific theory is related to the diversity of phenomena it can explain, and to its elegance and simplicity (see Occam's razor). As additional scientific evidence is gathered, a scientific theory may be rejected or modified if it does not fit the new empirical findings; in such circumstances, a more accurate theory is then desired. In certain cases, the less-accurate unmodified scientific theory can still be treated as a theory if it is useful (due to its sheer simplicity) as an approximation under specific conditions (e.g., Newton's laws of motion as an approximation to special relativity at velocities that are small relative to the speed of light).

Scientific theories are testable and make falsifiable predictions. They describe the causal elements responsible for a particular natural phenomenon, and are used to explain and predict aspects of the physical universe or specific areas of inquiry (e.g., electricity, chemistry, astronomy). Scientists use theories as a foundation to gain further scientific knowledge, as well as to accomplish goals such as inventing technology or curing disease. Wikipedia.

46. **Sir Karl Raimund Popper** CH FBA FRS (28 July 1902 – 17 September 1994) was an Austrian-British philosopher and professor. He is generally regarded as one of the greatest philosophers of science of the 20th century. Popper is known for his rejection of the classical inductivist views on the scientific method, in favor of empirical falsification: A theory in the empirical sciences can never be proven, but it can be falsified, meaning that it can and should be scrutinized by decisive experiments. Wikipedia.

47. The **Big Bang** theory is the prevailing cosmological model for the universe from the earliest known periods through its subsequent large-scale evolution. The model accounts for the fact that the universe expanded from a very high density and high temperature state and offers a comprehensive explanation for a broad range of phenomena, including the abundance of light elements, the cosmic microwave background, large scale structure and Hubble's Law. If the known laws of physics are extrapolated to the highest density regime, the result is a singularity which is typically associated with the Big Bang. Detailed measurements of the expansion rate of the universe place this moment at approximately 13.8 billion years ago, which is thus considered the age of the universe. After the initial expansion, the universe cooled

297

sufficiently to allow the formation of subatomic particles, and later simple atoms. Giant clouds of these primordial elements later coalesced through gravity in halos of dark matter, eventually forming the stars and galaxies visible today. Wikipedia.

48. Surtsey is the southernmost point of Iceland. It was formed in a volcanic eruption, which began 130 metres (426 ft) below sea level, and reached the surface on 14 November 1963. The eruption lasted until 5th June 1967, when the island reached its maximum size of 2.7 km^2 (1.0 sq mi). Wikipedia.

49. A **galaxy** is a gravitationally bound system of stars, stellar remnants, interstellar gas, dust, and dark matter. The word galaxy is derived from the Greek *galaxias* (γαλαξίας), literally "milky", a reference to the Milky Way. Galaxies range in size from dwarfs with just a few billion (10^9) stars to giants with one hundred trillion (10^{14}) stars, each orbiting its galaxy's center of mass. Wikipedia.

50. The **Sun** is the star at the center of the Solar System. It is a nearly perfect sphere of hot plasma, with internal convective motion that generates a magnetic field via a dynamo process. It is by far the most important source of energy for life on Earth. Its diameter is about 109 times that of Earth, and its mass is about 330,000 times that of Earth, accounting for about 99.86% of the total mass of the Solar System. About three quarters of the Sun's mass consists of hydrogen (~73%); the rest is mostly helium (~25%), with much smaller quantities of heavier elements, including oxygen, carbon, neon, and iron. Wikipedia.

51. https://science.nasa.gov/science-news/science-at-nasa/2003/02oct_goldilocks/

52. Sir Patrick Moore, presenter of The Sky at Night was fond of deprecatingly saying, 'Why should we expect to find extra-terrestrial intelligence? We haven't found it on Earth!' Personal observation.

53. **Gravitational waves** are ripples in the curvature of spacetime that propagate as waves at the speed of light, generated in certain gravitational interactions that propagate outward from their source. On February 11, 2016, the LIGO Scientific Collaboration and Virgo

298

Collaboration teams announced that they had made the first observation of gravitational waves, originating from a pair of merging black holes using the Advanced LIGO detectors. On June 15, 2016, a second detection of gravitational waves from coalescing black holes was announced. Wikipedia.

54. The **Higgs boson** is an elementary particle in the Standard Model of particle physics. It is the quantum excitation of the **Higgs field**, a fundamental field of crucial importance to particle physics theory first suspected to exist in the 1960s. On 4 July 2012, the discovery of a new particle with a mass between 125 and 127 GeV/c^2 was announced; physicists suspected that it was the Higgs boson. Wikipedia

55. **Osborne House** is a former royal residence in East Cowes, Isle of Wight, United Kingdom. The house was built between 1845 and 1851 for Queen Victoria and Prince Albert as a summer home and rural retreat. Prince Albert designed the house himself in the style of an Italian Renaissance palazzo. Wikipedia.

56.   https://www.theguardian.com/world/2005/oct/07/iraq.usa

57. The **Angel Moroni** (/moʊˈroʊnaɪ/) is, in Mormonism, an angel who visited Joseph Smith on numerous occasions, beginning on September 21, 1823. According to Smith, the angel was the guardian of the golden plates, which Latter Day Saints believe were the source material for the Book of Mormon, buried in a hill near Smith's home in western New York. Wikipedia.

58. **William Blake** (28 November 1757 – 12 August 1827) was an English poet, painter, and printmaker. Largely unrecognised during his lifetime, Blake is now considered a seminal figure in the history of the poetry and visual arts of the Romantic Age. Although Blake was considered mad by contemporaries for his idiosyncratic views, he is held in high regard by later critics for his expressiveness and creativity, and for the philosophical and mystical undercurrents within his work. Wikipedia.

59. **Prosopagnosia,** also called **face blindness,** is a cognitive disorder of face perception where the ability to recognize familiar faces, including one's own face (self-recognition), is impaired, while other aspects of

299

visual processing (e.g., object discrimination) and intellectual functioning (e.g., decision making) remain intact. The term originally referred to a condition following acute brain damage (acquired prosopagnosia), but a congenital or developmental form of the disorder also exists, which may affect up to 2.5% of the population. Wikipedia.

60. **Dr. Loftus** continues to stand by her own research into false memory. In describing that research, she identified two primary research paradigms that she studies in her memory laboratory at the University of California at Irvine. The first paradigm, which she calls the 'misinformation' paradigm involves testing research subjects on a specific event and seeing how accurate their memory for that event is afterward. The second paradigm, focusing on implanting false memories, involves bringing subjects in and asking suggestive questions and seeing whether that influences recall of past events. As she concludes in describing her research, "We've done hundreds of experiments involving thousands of subjects showing that it's relatively easy to change people's memory of the details of an event that they've actually experienced" Psychologytoday.com

61. It is often said that in 1694, while observing human sperm through a microscope, Hartsoeker believed that he saw tiny men inside the sperm, which he called homunculi or animalcules. However, he only postulated their existence as part of his Spermist theory of conception and never claimed to have seen them. Wikipedia.

62. **The 'Canali' and the First Martians** In the 1800s, observatories with larger and larger telescopes were built around the world. In 1877, Giovanni Virginio Schiaparelli (1835-1910), director of the Brera Observatory in Milan, began mapping and naming areas on Mars. He named the Martian "seas" and "continents" (dark and light areas) with names from historic and mythological sources. He saw channels on Mars and called them "canali." Canali means channels, but it was mistranslated into "canals" implying intelligent life on Mars. https://nasa.gov/audience/forstudents/postsecondary/

63. **Lawrence Maxwell Krauss** (born 27 May 1954) is an American

theoretical physicist and cosmologist who is Foundation Professor of the School of Earth and Space Exploration at Arizona State University, and director of its Origins Project. He is known as an advocate of the public understanding of science, of public policy based on sound empirical data, of scientific skepticism and of science education, and works to reduce the influence of what he opines as superstition and religious dogma in popular culture. Krauss is the author of several bestselling books, including *The Physics of Star Trek* (1995) and *A Universe from Nothing* (2012), and he chairs the *Bulletin of the Atomic Scientists* Board of Sponsors. Wikipedia.

64. Zeus was the god of the sky and ruler of the Olympian gods. He overthrew his father, Cronus, and then drew lots with his brothers Poseidon and Hades, in order to decide who would succeed their father on the throne. Zeus won the draw and became the supreme ruler of the gods, as well as lord of the sky and rain. His weapon was a thunderbolt which he hurled at those who displeased or defied him, especially liars and oathbreakers. www.greekmythology.com

65. In physics, **string theory** is a theoretical framework in which the point-like particles of particle physics are replaced by one-dimensional objects called strings. It describes how these strings propagate through space and interact with each other. On distance scales larger than the string scale, a string looks just like an ordinary particle, with its mass, charge, and other properties determined by the vibrational state of the string. In string theory, one of the many vibrational states of the string corresponds to the graviton, a quantum mechanical particle that carries gravitational force. Thus string theory is a theory of quantum gravity. Wikipedia.

66. The **multiverse** (or **meta-universe**) is the hypothetical set of possible universes, including the universe in which we live. Together, these universes comprise everything that exists: the entirety of space, time, matter, energy, and the physical laws and constants that describe them. The various universes within the multiverse are called "parallel universes", "other universes" or "alternative universes." Wikipedia.

67. **The President, Council and Fellows of the Royal Society of London for Improving Natural Knowledge**, commonly known as the **Royal Society**, is a learned society for science and is possibly the oldest such society still in existence. Founded in November 1660, it was granted a royal charter by King Charles II as "The Royal Society". The Society is the United Kingdom's and Commonwealth of Nations' Academy of Sciences and fulfills a number of roles; promoting science and its benefits, recognizing excellence in science, supporting outstanding science, providing scientific advice for policy, fostering international and global cooperation, education and public engagement. Wikipedia.

68. Dr. B. Stanley Pons, professor of chemistry at the University of Utah, and his colleague, Dr. Martin Fleischmann of the University of Southampton in England, touched off a furor by asserting on March 23 1989 in Salt Lake City that they had achieved nuclear fusion in a jar of water at room temperature.

     At a news conference today, nine of the leading speakers were asked if they would now rule the Utah claim as dead. Eight said yes, and one, Dr. Johann Rafelski of the University of Arizona, withheld judgment. Top physicists directed angry attacks at Dr. Pons and Dr. Fleischmann, calling them incompetent, reciting sarcastic verses about their claims and complaining that they had refused to provide details needed for follow-up experiments. A West European expert said "essentially all" West European attempts to duplicate cold fusion had failed. http://partners.nytimes.com

69. I drank a bottle of wine last night then, later, in the toilet, it turned into water! Am I the Anti-Christ?

70. References: http://tinyurl.com/m8wcmly and http://tinyurl.com/hndgfbo

71. Water is made up of hydrogen ions (H^+) linked to hydroxyl ions (OH^-) to form H_2O. The molecular formula for water is H_2O. From this formula and the atomic weights for hydrogen and oxygen you can calculate that the molecular weight of water is approximately 18.
     http://tinyurl.com/4kyphjm

Sam Harris said: 'Water is two parts hydrogen & one part oxygen. What if someone says 'Well that's not how I choose to think about water?' All we can do is appeal to scientific values. And if he doesn't share those values, the conversation is over. If someone doesn't value evidence, what evidence are you going to provide that they should value it? If someone doesn't value logic what logical argument could you provide to show the importance of logic?

72. The computer program first studied common patterns that are repeated in past games, Demis Hassabis, DeepMind chief executive explained to the BBC. "After it's learned that, it's got to reasonable standards by looking at professional games. It then played itself, different versions of itself millions and millions of times and each time get incrementally slightly better - it learns from its mistakes" Learning and improving from its own matchplay experience means the super computer is now even stronger than when it beat the European champion late last year.

http://tinyurl.com/h9jyrv5

73. The Euthyphro dilemma is found in Plato's dialogue *Euthyphro*, in which Socrates asks Euthyphro, "Is the pious (τὸ ὅσιον) loved by the gods because it is pious, or is it pious because it is loved by the gods?" The dilemma has had a major effect on the philosophical theism of the monotheistic religions, but in a modified form: "Is what is morally good commanded by God because it is morally good, or is it morally good because it is commanded by God?" Ever since Plato's original discussion, this question has presented a problem for some theists, though others have thought it a false dilemma, and it continues to be an object of theological and philosophical discussion today. Wikipedia.

76. The countries with the highest murder rates (one of the ten most important sins) are all highly religious Christian countries. The ten countries with the highest murder rates in the world are Brazil (25.2), Democratic Republic of the Congo (28.3), Trinidad and Tobago (28.3), Colombia (30.8), South Africa (31), Jamaica (39.3), Guatemala (39.9), El Salvador (41.2), Venezuela (53.7), and Honduras (90.4). The numbers in brackets are the number of intentional homicides per year

per 100,000 of population (latest available data). By comparison, the 10 countries with the lowest murder rates are Singapore, Japan, Kuwait, Hong Kong, Bahrain, Indonesia, Switzerland, Algeria, Slovenia and Sweden. Murder rates in these countries range from 0.2 to 0.7 per year per 100,000 of population. These countries have Muslims, Buddhists and 'atheists' in the majority - none of them are majority Christian countries. (Data compiled by Bill Flavell)

77. Jerusalem: The concept of Jerusalem as an open city negates the existence of any deep division in Jerusalem. Thick ethnic-national, political, community, religious, historical, and cultural walls separate the Jewish from the Arab (Muslim) side of the city. http://tinyurl.com/j3y9qja David Zohar says:

> Please note that 'god'/Allah/Elohim/Jehovah etc was a very poor town planner. Instead of separating religious foci of pilgrimage we see the opposite. In the city of Jerusalem where I live, Jewish, Moslem and Christian "Holy Places" are piled together in a mediaeval town in very close proximity leading to endless quarrels, fights and murders.

> Stabbings of pilgrims are commonplace. It is not safe to visit the Old City where most of these traditional places are to be found, and of course the inter-religious arguments provide ample fuel for endless Arab hostility towards Israel.

Belfast: A 'peace gate' has been opened in the barrier that divides Belfast's Alexandra Park, allowing Catholics and Protestants to mix – during the day at least. But a walk to survey the city's 99 peace walls offers vivid evidence of communities riven by hatred. http://tinyurl.com/zypa92mA

76. A recently discovered type of neuron--called a mirror neuron--could help explain how we learn through mimicry and why we empathize with others. http://tinyurl.com/mx5pwm4

77. **Social Darwinism** is a name given to various phenomena emerging in the second half of the 19th century, trying to apply biological concepts of natural selection and survival of the fittest in human society. The

304

term itself emerged in the 1880s. The term *Social Darwinism* gained widespread currency when used after 1944 by opponents of these earlier concepts. The majority of those who have been categorized as social Darwinists did not identify themselves by such a label. Ever wondered how many Christians supported eugenics? Religious leaders who embraced this supposed support for their social-gospel programs and who became involved in eugenics 'included Protestants of nearly every denomination, Jews and Catholics, and they overwhelmingly represented the liberal wings of their respective faiths. They were the ministers, priests, and rabbis who were inspired by the developments of modern science and accepted much of the new historical criticism of the Bible. Supporters ranged from high-ranking clerics to small-town ministers in the Methodist, Unitarian, Congregational, Protestant Episcopal, Baptist and Presbyterian churches.' Thus, in the early decades of the 20th century, 'clerics, rabbis and lay leaders wrote books and articles about eugenics, joined eugenics organizations ... and adopted eugenic solutions to the social problems that beset their communities. They explored the eugenic implications of the biblical Ten Commandments and investigated the hereditary lessons embedded in the parables of Jesus.' Many churches ran eugenics education classes. In 1910, psychologist Stanley Hall, wrote in the journal *Religious Education*, 'The entire Old Testament from the myth of Eden to the latest prophets needs a new eugenics exegesis.' In 1912, the Rev. Walter Sumner, Dean of the Episcopal Cathedral of Saints Peter and Paul in Chicago, required that couples wanting to be married in the cathedral must produce a eugenics health certificate. A physician had to attest that they were 'normal physically and mentally, and have neither an incurable nor communicable disease.' Some denominations approved and copied this procedure; others e.g. some Presbyterians, did not. Catholics mostly did not, as they regarded marriage as a sacrament to be regulated only by the church. In 1926, hundreds of preachers took part in a 'eugenics sermon contest' sponsored by the American Eugenics Society. Rosen comments, 'In eugenics, these men found a faith stronger than their Christianity, fulfilling Francis Galton's hopes of replacing religion with eugenics.' (from Wikipedia)

78. Several doctors have given estimates of the number of deaths that occur each year. Douglas Gairdner reported 16-19 actual deaths a year in England and Wales from neonatal circumcisions in the 1940s. Sydney Gellis believed that "there are more deaths from complications of circumcision than from cancer of the penis. There are various figures for the number of deaths from penile cancer ranging from 200 to 480 deaths per year. Robert Baker estimated 229 deaths per year from circumcision in the United States. Bollinger estimated that approximately 119 infant boys die from circumcision-related each year in the U.S. (1.3% of all male neonatal deaths from all causes). Doctors are highly motivated to conceal the true cause of circumcision death. Neonatal circumcision has no medical indication and is now considered to be an unnecessary non-therapeutic operation. It is unethical to carry out such operations on minors who cannot consent for themselves.
http://www.cirp.org/library/death/

79. American writer Max Ehrmann (1872–1945) wrote the prose poem "Desiderata" in 1927. In 1956, the Reverend Frederick Kates, rector of Saint Paul's Church in Baltimore, Maryland, included *Desiderata* in a compilation of devotional materials for his congregation. Wikipedia.

80. **Santa Claus**, also known as **Saint Nicholas**, **Saint Nick**, **Kris Kringle**, **Father Christmas**, or simply **Santa** (**Santy** in Hiberno-English), is a legendary figure of Western Christian culture who is said to bring gifts to the homes of well-behaved ("good" or "nice") children on Christmas Eve (24 December) and the early morning hours of Christmas Day (25 December). The modern Santa Claus grew out of traditions surrounding the historical Saint Nicholas, a fourth-century Greek bishop and gift-giver of Myra, the British figure of Father Christmas, the Dutch figure of *Sinterklaas* (himself based on Saint Nicholas), the German figure of the Christkind (a fabulized Christ Child), and the holidays of Twelfth Night and Epiphany and their associated figures of the Three Kings (based on the gift-giving Magi of the Nativity) and Befana. Some maintain

306

Santa Claus also absorbed elements of the Germanic god Wodan, who was associated with the pagan midwinter event of Yule and led the Wild Hunt, a ghostly procession through the sky. Wikipedia.

81. **"The Emperor's New Clothes"** (Danish: *Kejserens nye Klæder*) is a short tale written by Danish author Hans Christian Andersen about two weavers who promise an emperor a new suit of clothes that they say is invisible to those who are unfit for their positions, stupid, or incompetent. When the Emperor parades before his subjects in his new clothes, no one dares to say that they don't see any suit of clothes on him for fear that they will be seen as "unfit for their positions, stupid, or incompetent". Finally, a child cries out, "But he isn't wearing anything at all!" The tale has been translated into over 100 languages. Wikipedia.

82. The Goddess of Chocolate/Cocoa had humble but honorable origins as a Mayan Goddess. Named Ixcacao, she was an ancient fertility goddess, an earth goddess in a matriarchal society where gathering crops and seeing to it that everyone was fed was woman's work.
http://tinyurl.com/gltaubg

83. In Roman mythology, **Cloacina** (Latin, *cloaca*: "sewer" or "drain") was the goddess who presided over the Cloaca Maxima ("Great Drain"), the main trunk of the system of sewers in Rome. Wikipedia.

84. ps://en.wikipedia.org/wiki/List_of_religious_populations

85. Fraud Act 2006

(1) A person is guilty of fraud if he is in breach of any of the sections listed in subsection (2) (which provide for different ways of committing the offence).

(2) The sections are—

(a) section 2 (fraud by false representation),

(b) section 3 (fraud by failing to disclose information), and

(c) section 4 (fraud by abuse of position).

(3) A person who is guilty of fraud is liable—

(a) on summary conviction, to imprisonment for a term not exceeding 12 months or to a fine not exceeding the statutory maximum (or to both);

(b) conviction on indictment, to imprisonment for a term not exceeding 10 years or to a fine (or to both).

86. Ancient Egyptian gods http://tinyurl.com/jor83jn

87. Churches are tax exempt https://www.irs.gov/charities-non-profits/churches-religious-organizations and Bishops sit in the UK government https://en.wikipedia.org/wiki/Lords_Spiritual

88. The **John Templeton Foundation** is a philanthropic organization with a spiritual or religious inclination that funds inter-disciplinary research about human purpose and ultimate reality. It is usually referred to simply as the **Templeton Foundation**. It was established in 1987 by investor and philanthropist Sir John Templeton; his son John Templeton, Jr. took over the presidency until his death in 2015. Heather Templeton Dill became president in June, 2015. Wikipedia.

89. The first marriage of Henry VIII of England to Catherine of Aragon required a papal dispensation as it breached canon law on Affinity because she was the widow of Henry's elder brother Arthur, Prince of Wales. Wikipedia.

90. **Malaria** is a mosquito-borne infectious disease affecting humans and other animals caused by parasitic protozoans (a group of single-celled microorganisms) belonging to the *Plasmodium* type. Malaria causes symptoms that typically include fever, fatigue, vomiting, and headaches. In severe cases it can cause yellow skin, seizures, coma, or death. Wikipedia.

91. *Loa loa* **filariasis** is a skin and eye disease caused by the nematode worm *Loa loa*. Humans contract this disease through the bite of a deer fly or mango fly (*Chrysops* spp), the vectors for *Loa loa*. The adult *Loa loa* filarial worm migrates throughout the subcutaneous tissues of humans, occasionally crossing into subconjunctival tissues of the eye where it can be easily observed. Wikipedia.

92. **Galileo Galilei** (Italian pronunciation: [galiˈlɛːo galiˈlɛi]; 15 February 1564 – 8 January 1642) was an Italian polymath: astronomer, physicist, engineer, philosopher, and mathematician, he played a major role in the scientific revolution of the seventeenth century. Wikipedia.

93. **Giordano Bruno** (Italian: [dʒorˈdano ˈbruno]; Latin: *Iordanus Brunus Nolanus*; 1 January 1548 – 17 February 1600), born **Filippo Bruno**, was an Italian Dominican friar, philosopher, mathematician, poet, and cosmological theorist. He is remembered for his cosmological theories, which conceptually extended the then novel Copernican model. Wikipedia.

94. Ptolemy's model, like those of his predecessors, was geocentric and was almost universally accepted until the appearance of simpler heliocentric models during the scientific revolution. His *Planetary Hypotheses* went beyond the mathematical model of the *Almagest* to present a physical realization of the universe as a set of nested spheres, in which he used the epicycles of his planetary model to compute the dimensions of the universe. He estimated the Sun was at an average distance of 1,210 Earth radii, while the radius of the sphere of the fixed stars was 20,000 times the radius of the Earth. Wikipedia.

95. The word *Allah* has been used by Arabs of different religions since pre-Islamic times. More specifically, it has been used as a term to refer to God by Muslims (both Arab and non-Arab) and Arab Christians. It is now mainly used by Muslims and Arab Christians to refer to God. Wikipedia.

96. **Yahweh** (/ˈjɑːhweɪ/, or often /ˈjɑːweɪ/ in English; Hebrew: יהוה‎) was the national god of the Iron Age kingdoms of Israel (Samaria) and Judah. His origins are unknown, although they reach back to the early Iron Age and even the Late Bronze: his name may have begun as an epithet of El, head of the Bronze Age Canaanite pantheon, but the earliest plausible mentions are in Egyptian texts that place him among the nomads of the southern Transjordan. Wikipedia.

97. **Jesus** (born some time between 7 and 3 BC, died between 30 and 33 AD), also referred to as **Jesus of Nazareth**, was a Jewish teacher and reformer of religion who has become the central figure of Christianity. Christians respect and adore him, his life, and his being so much that they declare and worship him as a "god". Most historians agree that he was a Jew from a place called Judea, in a town called Nazareth, in

what is now Israel. They also agree that he was thought of as a teacher and a healer, and that he was baptized by John the Baptist. The Quran claims that Jesus was a Muslim. Wikipedia.

98. **Ganesha** (/gəˈneɪʃə/; Sanskrit: गणेश, *Gaṇeśa*; also known as **Ganapati** and **Vinayaka**, is one of the best-known and most worshipped deities in the Hindu pantheon. His image is found throughout India, Sri Lanka and Nepal. Hindu sects worship him regardless of affiliations. Devotion to Ganesha is widely diffused and extends to Jains and Buddhists. Although he is known by many attributes, Ganesha's elephant head makes him easy to identify. Wikipedia.

99. **The Clergy Project (TCP)** is an international non-profit organization based in the United States that helps current and former religious leaders who no longer believe in the supernatural. The group's focus is to provide a secure, private online community of forums for its participants, while also providing further assistance as able, such as aiding members in employment transition. Wikipedia.

100. The Sea of Faith Network explores the implications of accepting religion as a human creation and promotes the validity of creative, human-centred religion. http://www.sofn.org.uk

RECIPE FOR WAR OR TERRORISM

Take two different god hypotheses
Back them by opinion, not evidence
Enforce them with laws of 'blasphemy' and 'apostasy'
Support them with emotional argument
Leading to egoistical and insulting disagreement
Followed by division and demonisation
Whenever two such mind-sets come head to head
Conflict is almost guaranteed

A child's world is a wonderful place, no wonder so many of us
don't want to leave it...

"There are, in fact, two things, Science and opinion;
the former begets knowledge, the latter ignorance."
Hippocrates of Cos (2000 yrs ago)

"I don't believe in Science.
Science is our defense against belief."
J. Allan HOBSON,
Emeritus Professor of Psychiatry, Harvard Medical School

"Science is not perfect. It's often misused. It's only a tool, but it's
the best tool we have. Self correcting, ever changing, applicable
to everything, with this tool, we vanquish the impossible."
Carl SAGAN

Is God willing to prevent evil, but not able?
Then He is not omnipotent.
Is He able but not willing?
Then He is malevolent.
Is He both willing & able?
Then whence cometh evil?
Is He neither willing nor able?
Then why call Him God?
Epicurus (c 341 – c. 270 BCE)

Science posits a process, theists posit a being.
Now where do they reconcile?
Carl William RAINES I

www.ingramcontent.com/pod-product-compliance
Lightning Source LLC
Chambersburg PA
CBHW070019100426
42740CB00013B/2560